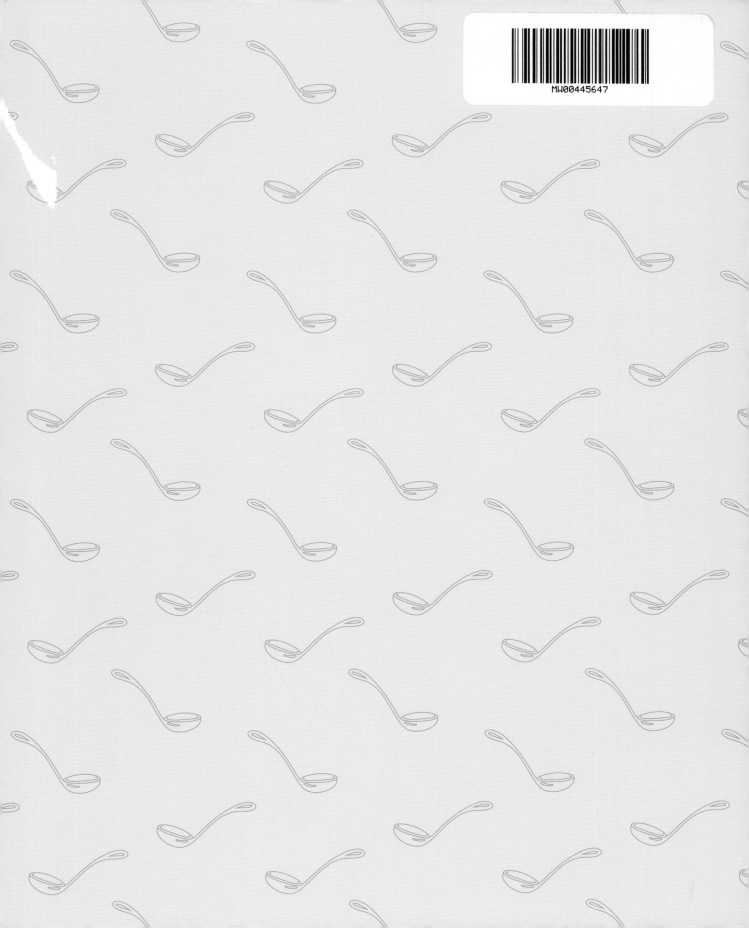

THE COMPLETE
SOUP
COOKBOOK

THE COMPLETE SOUP COOKBOOK

Over 200 Satisfying Recipes for Every Appetite

13-Digit ISBN: 978-1-64643-278-3
10-Digit ISBN: 1-64643-278-9

This book may be ordered by mail from the publisher. Please include $5.99 for postage and handling. Please support your local bookseller first!

Books published by Cider Mill Press Book Publishers are available at special discounts for bulk purchases in the United States by corporations, institutions, and other organizations. For more information, please contact the publisher.

Cider Mill Press Book Publishers
"Where Good Books Are Ready for Press"
501 Nelson Place
Nashville, TN 37214
Visit us online!
cidermillpress.com

Typography: Adobe Garamond Pro, Gotham, Farmhand, Avenir, Linotype Centennial

Image Credits: Images on pages 21, 27, 30-31, 41, 49, 71, 83, 92, 96, 99, 104, 122, 125, 137, 142, 145-146, 150, 166, 181-182, 217, 223, 225, 265, 269, 270, 273-274, 294-295, 300, 303-304, 317-318, 330, 334, 336, 342 used under official license from Shutterstock.com

All other images courtesy of Cider Mill Press.

Printed in China

Front cover image: Tunisian Spiced Butternut Squash Soup, page 224
Back cover image: Crab & Oyster Gumbo, page 155

2 3 4 5 6 7 8 9 0

THE COMPLETE
SOUP
COOKBOOK

Over 200 Satisfying Recipes for Every Appetite

CIDER MILL
PRESS

BOOK
PUBLISHERS

TABLE of CONTENTS

❋ ❋ ❋

SOUP: THE ONLY UNIVERSAL DISH

❈ ❈ ❈

Soup is universal. The world contains countless cuisines, techniques, and ingredients. But there is one thing that bonds them all—every single culture has some form of soup. As human culture took shape, so did soup, starting in China in 20,000 BCE. The scorch marks on a ceramic bowl found in a cave in Jiangxi Province indicated that whatever was eaten out of this bowl had been cooked over fire.

Broths show up in the historical record around the year 1000 CE, and in the fifteenth century, soup dishes known as potages became a staple in the diets of peasants around the world. In fact, soups are such a vital part of what we eat that the word stems from the same Latin word that supper does: suppare.

The best way to cook, and the most efficient use of fire's precious heat, is boiling. Boiling kills any potential parasites in animal proteins, preserves nutrients, increases the amount of antioxidants, and makes food easier to chew. Most important, the cooking liquid retains meat's tasty juices, which would be lost if cooked over an open flame.

Soup came to be known as a meal that promotes healing. Old medical textbooks read more like diet books. In China, snakes were used to make soups that were believed to help with joint pain. The meat of a strong animal was thought to strengthen a weak man. Of course, there is the age-old belief in chicken soup's healing capabilities. This stems from the ancient Greeks, who recommended the meat of hens and roosters, and broth made from their bones, for many treatments.

As it turns out, scientists have confirmed that this was not just an ancient superstition. Chicken contains a compound called carnosine that actually slows or blocks the migration of white blood cells, which reduces the amount of inflammation in the respiratory tract that results from the common cold. Researchers have also found that chicken soup may improve one's ability to deflect a virus and weaken it upon entry into the body. On top of all this, it also allows mucus to escape the body more freely, which keeps airways clear and eases the effects of congestion. So, with chicken soup, as with most things, it turns out that the ancient Greeks, and your mother, have it right.

Beyond the health benefits of soups, in times of emotional stress, they can evoke feelings of warmth, happiness, satisfaction, and human connection.

The recipes for soups and stews found in the following pages demonstrate the universal appeal of these comforting and delicious meals, sampling cuisines from around the world. There is a soup for everyone and every occasion in this book. So, get your spoons ready and dig in to this comprehensive collection. You won't be disappointed.

CHAPTER 1

STOCKS

In French cuisine, a basic stock is referred to as a fonds, which translates to "foundation." Some soups require the solid foundation a stock can provide, while others need nothing more than the proper combination of ingredients, time, and patience.

When you're preparing a stock, soup, or stew, resist the temptation to tinker and leave your seasoning until the end. Since there are a lot of salts and minerals naturally occurring in your ingredients, these will enter the soup as it cooks. Think of time and heat as doing the seasoning for you, as the flavor of almost every soup is indicative of the time invested.

A stock is traditionally a base for broths and consommés made from the bones and carcasses of a protein source (vegetable stock is an obvious exception), and often features vegetables and aromatics. It is important that the bones are cooked for hours so that every last bit of flavor makes its way into the stock.

There are white stocks and brown stocks. The former is made from the bones of white meat, such as chicken, and lighter colored vegetables. Brown stocks are made from the bones of darker meats, such as beef.

This cannot be emphaszied enough: try and save the bones from what you cook at home to use in your stocks. You can buy bones from a butcher or a fishmonger, but you're paying money to haul away their garbage. If you happen to be on good terms with your butcher or fishmonger and can get the bones for free, go right ahead. (There is one good thing about buying your bones from the butcher: you can have them cut there, which will maximize the amount of gelatin and flavor that can be extracted.)

If you have time—and, to be a master of soup, you'd better—then you can get more flavor and more stock out of the same group of bones. Here's how: when your first stock is finished, strain it, set the bones, vegetables, and aromatics aside, and place everything in the refrigerator overnight. The next day, reuse the bones, vegetables, and aromatics, and make a second stock.

When the second stock is done, strain it and chill. Naturally, this second stock won't contain as much flavor or gelatin as the first, which is why, on the third day, you're going to combine them. You'll want to reduce this combo stock nice and slowly, making sure to skim as much fat and as many impurities out as you can. No matter what, you won't be able to get them all, which is why it's important to refrigerate your stock prior to using or freezing. When the stock is cold, the fat and the remaining impurities will settle on top, making them easy to remove.

If the fat is from chicken or duck meat, feel free to save it, or freeze it, for later use. This is not the traditional way of rendering these fats, but it yields the same results.

While making your own stock is essential to making great soup, stocks are available at your local grocery store. And some of them are actually decent. But nothing store bought will replicate the stock you will produce at home—so save the packaged stuff for absolute emergencies.

To keep those emergencies from occurring, you'll want to purchase a large stockpot. But don't go too large—for a home range, you don't need anything larger than a 16-quart stockpot, since a majority of stoves won't burn hot enough to handle a stock pot larger than this.

The word "broth" is often used to describe stocks; even among chefs the terms are often interchangeable. But they are technically different: broths are stocks that have been enhanced with whole pieces of meat, vegetables, and, often, the addition of carbohydrates such as potatoes, pasta, or beans. Think of a broth as a finalized product, rather than a concentrate to be dressed up.

TIPS:

Stocks can stay in a freezer for up to six months.

These are large recipes, which can easily be reduced to half or one-quarter the amount. However, as the same amount of time is required, it is recommended to make a larger quantity and save some for the future.

VEAL, BEEF, OR LAMB STOCK

YIELD: **6 QUARTS**

ACTIVE TIME: **30 MINUTES**

TOTAL TIME: **5 HOURS AND 20 MINUTES**

INGREDIENTS

10 LBS. VEAL, BEEF, OR LAMB BONES

½ CUP VEGETABLE OIL

1 LEEK, TRIMMED AND CAREFULLY WASHED, CUT INTO 1-INCH PIECES

1 LARGE YELLOW ONION, UNPEELED, CLEANED ROOT, CUT INTO 1-INCH PIECES

2 LARGE CARROTS, PEELED AND CUT INTO 1-INCH PIECES

1 CELERY STALK WITH LEAVES, CUT INTO 1-INCH PIECES

10 QUARTS WATER

8 PARSLEY SPRIGS

5 THYME SPRIGS

2 BAY LEAVES

1 TEASPOON PEPPERCORNS

1 TEASPOON SALT

8 OZ. TOMATO PASTE

DIRECTIONS

1. Preheat the oven to 350°F.

2. Lay the bones on a flat baking tray, place in oven, and cook for 30 to 45 minutes, until they are golden brown. Remove and set aside.

3. Meanwhile, in a large stockpot, add the vegetable oil and warm over low heat. Add the vegetables and cook until any additional moisture has evaporated. This allows the flavor of the vegetables to become concentrated.

4. Add the water to the stockpot. Add the bones, aromatics, and tomato paste to the stockpot, raise heat to high, and bring to a boil.

5. Reduce heat so that the stock simmers and cook for a minimum of 2 hours. Skim fat and impurities from the top as the stock cooks. As for when to stop cooking the stock, let the flavor be the judge. I typically like to cook for 4 to 5 hours total.

6. When the stock is finished cooking, strain through a fine strainer or cheesecloth. Place stock in refrigerator to chill.

7. Once cool, skim the fat layer from the top and discard. Use immediately, refrigerate, or freeze.

YIELD: **6 QUARTS**

ACTIVE TIME: **20 MINUTES**

TOTAL TIME: **5 HOURS AND 20 MINUTES**

CHICKEN STOCK

INGREDIENTS

10 LBS. CHICKEN CARCASSES AND/
OR STEWING CHICKEN PIECES

½ CUP VEGETABLE OIL

1 LEEK, TRIMMED AND CAREFULLY
WASHED, CUT INTO 1-INCH
PIECES

1 LARGE YELLOW ONION,
UNPEELED, CLEANED ROOT, CUT
INTO 1-INCH PIECES

2 LARGE CARROTS, CUT INTO
1-INCH PIECES

1 CELERY STALK WITH LEAVES, CUT
INTO 1-INCH PIECES

10 QUARTS WATER

1 TEASPOON SALT

8 PARSLEY SPRIGS

5 THYME SPRIGS

2 BAY LEAVES

1 TEASPOON PEPPERCORNS

DIRECTIONS

1. Preheat the oven to 350°F.

2. Lay the bones on a flat baking tray, place in oven, and cook for 30 to 45 minutes until they are golden brown. Remove and set aside.

3. Meanwhile, in a large stockpot, add the vegetable oil and warm over low heat. Add the vegetables and cook until any additional moisture has evaporated. This allows the flavor of the vegetables to become concentrated.

4. Add the water and the salt to the stockpot. Add the chicken carcasses and/or stewing pieces and the aromatics to the stockpot, raise heat to high, and bring to a boil.

5. Reduce heat so that the stock simmers and cook for a minimum of 2 hours. Skim fat and impurities from the top as the stock cooks. As for when to stop cooking the stock, let the flavor be the judge. I typically like to cook for 4 to 5 hours total.

6. When the stock is finished cooking, strain through a fine strainer or cheesecloth. Place stock in refrigerator to chill.

7. Once cool, skim the fat layer from the top and discard. Use immediately, refrigerate, or freeze.

CRAB STOCK

YIELD: **4 QUARTS**

ACTIVE TIME: **30 MINUTES**

TOTAL TIME: **2 TO 4 HOURS**

INGREDIENTS

2 TABLESPOONS VEGETABLE OIL

1 ONION, CHOPPED

1 CARROT, PEELED, ROUGHLY CHOPPED

1 CELERY STALK, ROUGHLY CHOPPED

3 LBS. CRAB LEGS, COOKED IN THE SHELL, MEAT REMOVED AND RESERVED, SHELLS USED IN STOCK

½ CUP WHITE WINE

4 TABLESPOONS TOMATO PASTE

2 THYME SPRIGS

2 PARSLEY SPRIGS

3 SPRIGS TARRAGON

1 BAY LEAF

½ TEASPOON BLACK PEPPERCORNS

1 TEASPOON SALT

8 CARDAMOM PODS

DIRECTIONS

1. In a large stockpot, add the vegetable oil and warm over low heat. Add the vegetables and cook until any additional moisture has evaporated. This will allow the flavor of the vegetables to become concentrated.

2. Add the crab shells, the remaining ingredients, and enough water to cover the shells by 1 inch.

3. Raise heat to high and bring to a boil. Reduce heat so that the stock simmers and cook for a minimum of 2 hours. Skim fat and impurities from the top as the stock cooks. As for when to stop cooking the stock, let the flavor be the judge. I typically like to cook for 4 hours total.

4. When the stock is finished cooking, strain through a fine strainer or cheesecloth. Place stock in refrigerator to chill.

5. Once cool, skim the fat layer from the top and discard. Use immediately, refrigerate, or freeze.

DASHI STOCK

INGREDIENTS

8 CUPS COLD WATER

2 OZ. KOMBU

1 CUP BONITO FLAKES

DIRECTIONS

1. In a medium saucepan, add the water and the kombu. Soak for 20 minutes, remove the kombu, and score gently with a knife.

2. Return the kombu to the saucepan and bring to a boil.

3. Remove the kombu as soon as the water boils, so that the stock doesn't become bitter.

4. Add the bonito flakes and return to a boil. Turn off heat and let stand.

5. Strain through a fine sieve and chill in refrigerator.

YIELD: **4 CUPS**

ACTIVE TIME: **15 MINUTES**

TOTAL TIME: **1 HOUR AND 15 MINUTES**

HAM STOCK

INGREDIENTS

12 OZ. HAM

6 CUPS WATER

2 GARLIC CLOVES, MINCED

1 ONION, CHOPPED

1 BAY LEAF

1 THYME SPRIG

DIRECTIONS

1. Combine all ingredients in a stockpot and bring to a boil.

2. Reduce heat so that the stock simmers and cook for 1 hour. Strain stock through a fine sieve and chill in refrigerator.

FISH STOCK

YIELD: **6 QUARTS**

ACTIVE TIME: **20 MINUTES**

TOTAL TIME: **3 HOURS AND 20 MINUTES**

INGREDIENTS

½ CUP VEGETABLE OIL

1 LEEK, TRIMMED AND CAREFULLY WASHED, CUT INTO 1-INCH PIECES

1 LARGE YELLOW ONION, UNPEELED, CLEANED ROOT, CUT INTO 1-INCH PIECES

2 LARGE CARROTS, CUT INTO 1-INCH PIECES

1 CELERY STALK WITH LEAVES, CUT INTO 1-INCH PIECES

10 LBS. WHITEFISH BODIES

8 PARSLEY SPRIGS

5 THYME SPRIGS

2 BAY LEAVES

1 TEASPOON PEPPERCORNS

1 TEASPOON SALT

10 QUARTS WATER

DIRECTIONS

1. In a large stockpot, add the vegetable oil and warm over low heat. Add the vegetables and cook until any additional moisture has evaporated. This will allow the flavor of the vegetables to become concentrated.

2. Add the whitefish bodies, the aromatics, the peppercorns, the salt, and the water to the pot.

3. Raise heat to high and bring to a boil. Reduce heat so that the stock simmers and cook for a minimum of 2 hours. Skim fat and impurities from the top as the stock cooks. As for when to stop cooking the stock, let the flavor be the judge. I typically like to cook for 2 to 3 hours total.

4. When the stock is finished cooking, strain through a fine strainer or cheesecloth. Place stock in refrigerator to chill.

5. Once cool, skim the fat layer from the top and discard. Use immediately, refrigerate, or freeze.

LOBSTER STOCK

YIELD: **8 CUPS**

ACTIVE TIME: **20 MINUTES**

TOTAL TIME: **4 HOURS AND 20 MINUTES**

INGREDIENTS

5 LBS. LOBSTER SHELLS AND BODIES

2 TABLESPOONS VEGETABLE OIL

1 LB. MIXED ROOT VEGETABLES (CARROT, LEEK, ONION, CELERY), CHOPPED

10 TOMATOES, CHOPPED

1 CUP V8

1 BUNCH THYME

1 BUNCH PARSLEY

1 BUNCH TARRAGON

1 BUNCH DILL

1 GARLIC CLOVE

2 CUPS WHITE WINE

DIRECTIONS

1. Preheat the oven to 350°F.

2. Lay the lobster bodies on a baking tray, place in oven, and cook for 30 to 45 minutes. Remove and set aside.

3. Meanwhile, in a large stockpot, add the vegetable oil and warm over low heat. Add the root vegetables and cook until any additional moisture has evaporated. This allows the flavor of the vegetables to become concentrated.

4. Add the lobster bodies, tomatoes, V8, herbs, garlic, and white wine to the stockpot. Add enough water to cover the shells, raise heat to high, and bring to a boil. Reduce heat so that the stock simmers and cook for a minimum of 2 hours. Skim fat and impurities from the top as the stock cooks. As for when to stop cooking the stock, let the flavor be the judge. I typically like to cook for 3 to 4 hours total.

5. When the stock is finished cooking, strain through a fine strainer or cheesecloth. Place stock in refrigerator to chill.

6. Once cool, skim the fat layer from the top and discard. Use immediately, refrigerate, or freeze.

MUSHROOM STOCK

YIELD: **6 CUPS**

ACTIVE TIME: **20 MINUTES**

TOTAL TIME: **3 HOURS AND 20 MINUTES**

INGREDIENTS

2 TABLESPOONS VEGETABLE OIL

3 LBS. MUSHROOMS

1 ONION, CHOPPED

1 GARLIC, MINCED

2 BAY LEAVES

1 TABLESPOON BLACK PEPPERCORNS

2 THYME SPRIGS

1 CUP WHITE WINE

8 CUPS WATER

DIRECTIONS

1. In a large stockpot, add the vegetable oil and mushrooms and cook over low heat for 30 to 40 minutes. The longer you cook the mushrooms, the better.

2. Add onion, garlic, bay leaves, peppercorns, and thyme and cook for 5 minutes.

3. Add the white wine, cook 5 minutes, and then add the water.

4. Bring to a boil, reduce heat so that stock simmers, and cook for 2 to 3 hours, until you are pleased with the taste.

VEGETABLE STOCK

YIELD: **6 CUPS**

ACTIVE TIME: **20 MINUTES**

TOTAL TIME: **2 HOURS AND 20 MINUTES**

INGREDIENTS

2 TABLESPOONS VEGETABLE OIL

2 LARGE LEEKS, TRIMMED AND CAREFULLY WASHED

2 LARGE CARROTS, PEELED AND SLICED

2 CELERY STALKS, SLICED

2 LARGE ONIONS, SLICED

3 GARLIC CLOVES, UNPEELED BUT SMASHED

2 PARSLEY SPRIGS

2 THYME SPRIGS

1 BAY LEAF

8 CUPS WATER

½ TEASPOON BLACK PEPPERCORNS

SALT, TO TASTE

DIRECTIONS

1. In a large stockpot, add the vegetable oil and the vegetables and garlic and cook over low heat until any additional moisture has evaporated. This will allow the flavor of the vegetables to become concentrated.

2. Add parsley, thyme, bay leaf, water, peppercorns, and salt. Raise heat to high and bring to a boil. Reduce heat so that the soup simmers and cook for 2 hours. Skim fat and impurities from the top as the stock cooks.

3. When the stock is finished cooking, strain through a fine strainer or cheesecloth. Place stock in refrigerator to chill.

4. Once cool, skim the fat layer from the top and discard. Use immediately, refrigerate, or freeze.

CHAPTER 2

CLASSICS

_____

The aromas from the kitchen, the flavors of comfort, the satisfaction of feeling full—these are the soups that remind you of home, no matter where you grew up.

AFRICAN PEANUT SOUP

YIELD: **4 SERVINGS**

ACTIVE TIME: **20 MINUTES**

TOTAL TIME: **1 HOUR**

INGREDIENTS

½ CUP NATURAL PEANUT BUTTER

2 TABLESPOONS TOMATO PASTE

6 CUPS CHICKEN STOCK

1 ONION, CHOPPED

1-INCH PIECE GINGER, PEELED AND MINCED

2 THYME SPRIGS, LEAVES REMOVED AND CHOPPED

1 BAY LEAF

⅛ TEASPOON CAYENNE PEPPER, OR TO TASTE

1 SWEET POTATO, PEELED AND CHOPPED

6 FRESH OKRA, SLICED

SALT AND PEPPER, TO TASTE

EDIBLE FLOWERS, FOR GARNISH

DIRECTIONS

1. In a medium saucepan, add the peanut butter and tomato paste. Slowly add the chicken stock, whisking constantly to keep lumps from forming.

2. Add the onion, ginger, thyme, bay leaf, and cayenne pepper.

3. Cook over medium heat and bring to a simmer. Cook for 30 minutes, stirring often.

4. Add the sweet potato and cook for 10 minutes. Add the okra and cook for an additional 5 minutes, or until the okra and sweet potato are tender.

5. Season with salt and pepper and serve warmed bowls with edible flowers.

AVGOLEMONO WITH ORZO SALAD

YIELD: **4 SERVINGS**

ACTIVE TIME: **45 MINUTES**

TOTAL TIME: **1 HOUR AND 15 MINUTES**

DIRECTIONS

1. Pour the stock into a large saucepan and bring to a boil.

2. Reduce the heat so that the stock simmers. Add the chicken thighs and cook for 20 minutes.

3. Remove the chicken thighs and set aside. Add the orzo and cook for 5 minutes.

4. Meanwhile, remove the meat from the chicken thighs, discard the skin and bones, and chop the meat into bite-sized pieces.

5. Strain the orzo from the stock and set aside. Return the stock to the pan and bring to a simmer.

6. In a mixing bowl, add the eggs and beat until frothy. Add the lemon juice and cold water and whisk. Add approximately ½ cup of the stock to bowl and stir constantly.

7. Add another cup of hot stock to the egg mixture and then add the contents of the bowl to the saucepan. Be careful not to let the stock boil once you add the egg mixture, otherwise it will curdle.

8. Add half of the cooked orzo and the chicken to the saucepan. Season with salt and pepper and ladle into warmed bowls. Garnish with parsley and lemon slices and serve with Orzo Salad.

ORZO SALAD

1. In a medium-sized mixing bowl, add the orzo, feta cheese, bell peppers, Kalamata olives, scallion, capers, garlic, parsley, and pine nuts and stir until combined.

2. In a small bowl, add the lemon juice, vinegar, mustard, and cumin and stir until combined. Gradually whisk in the olive oil and then add the dressing to the orzo mixture. Toss to blend, season with salt and pepper, cover, and refrigerate until ready to serve.

INGREDIENTS

6 CUPS CHICKEN STOCK

2 CHICKEN THIGHS

1 CUP ORZO PASTA

3 EGGS

1 TABLESPOON LEMON JUICE

1 TABLESPOON COLD WATER

SALT AND PEPPER, TO TASTE

LEMON SLICES, FOR GARNISH

PARSLEY, CHOPPED, FOR GARNISH

TO SERVE:

ORZO SALAD

ORZO SALAD

½ CUP OF ORZO, COOKED

¼ CUP CRUMBLED FETA CHEESE

¼ CUP CHOPPED RED BELL PEPPER

3 TABLESPOONS CHOPPED YELLOW
   BELL PEPPER

3 TABLESPOONS CHOPPED
   KALAMATA OLIVES

1 SCALLION, SLICED

1 TEASPOON CAPERS, DRAINED AND
   CHOPPED

1 TEASPOON MINCED GARLIC

1 TEASPOON CHOPPED PARSLEY
   LEAVES

1 TABLESPOON TOASTED AND
   CHOPPED PINE NUTS

2 TEASPOONS LEMON JUICE

1 TEASPOON WHITE WINE VINEGAR

1 TEASPOON DIJON MUSTARD

½ TEASPOON CUMIN

3 TABLESPOONS EXTRA-VIRGIN
   OLIVE OIL

SALT AND PEPPER, TO TASTE

BACON & PEA SOUP

YIELD: **6 SERVINGS**

ACTIVE TIME: **30 MINUTES**

TOTAL TIME: **1 HOUR**

INGREDIENTS

½ LB. BACON, DICED

4 TABLESPOONS UNSALTED BUTTER

1 ONION, DICED

3 CUPS PEAS

4 CUPS CHICKEN STOCK

DIRECTIONS

1. Add the bacon to a frying pan over medium heat and cook until browned. Remove the bacon and drain on a paper towel–lined plate.

2. Add butter to a saucepan over medium-low heat. When it begins to foam, add the onion and sauté until it turns soft and pale, about 6 minutes.

3. Add the peas and stock, bring to a boil, and then lower heat and simmer for 25 minutes.

4. Using an immersion blender, puree the soup and season to taste.

5. Serve in bowls topped with the cooked bacon.

BAJA TORTILLA SOUP

YIELD: **4 SERVINGS**

ACTIVE TIME: **25 MINUTES**

TOTAL TIME: **1 HOUR**

INGREDIENTS

6 TOMATILLOS, HUSKED AND RINSED WELL

3 MEDIUM HEIRLOOM TOMATOES

½ WHITE ONION, CHOPPED

2 GARLIC CLOVES, UNPEELED

1 JALAPEÑO CHILI PEPPER

2 TEASPOONS EXTRA-VIRGIN OLIVE OIL

1 TEASPOON SMOKED PAPRIKA

1 TEASPOON CHILI POWDER

1 TEASPOON CUMIN

SALT AND PEPPER, TO TASTE

6 CORN TORTILLAS

4 CUPS VEGETABLE STOCK

MARYLAND BLUE CRAB KNUCKLE MEAT, FOR GARNISH

LIME CREMA, FOR GARNISH

AVOCADO OIL, FOR GARNISH

FRESH CILANTRO, CHOPPED, FOR SERVING

FRIED TORTILLA STRIPS, FOR SERVING

DIRECTIONS

1. Preheat the oven to 375°F. In a mixing bowl, combine the tomatillos, tomatoes, onion, garlic, and jalapeño. Add the oil, smoked paprika, chili powder, cumin, salt, and pepper and stir until the vegetables are coated.

2. Transfer the mixture to a baking sheet. Place the tortillas on a separate baking sheet. Place the pans in the oven and roast until the tomatillos and tomatoes are charred and starting to collapse, and the tortillas are toasted and crisp, about 20 minutes. Remove from the oven and let the vegetables cool slightly. When cool enough to handle, chop the vegetables roughly, making sure to peel the garlic cloves and remove the stem and seeds from the jalapeño before chopping them.

3. Place the stock in a medium saucepan and bring it to a boil. Add the vegetables and any juices to the pan. Add the tortillas and simmer the soup until the flavors are combined, about 5 minutes.

4. Transfer the soup to a blender and puree until smooth. Ladle the soup into warm bowls and garnish each portion with some crabmeat, crema, and avocado oil. Serve with cilantro and fried tortilla strips.

INGREDIENTS

SHORT RIBS

2 TABLESPOONS AVOCADO OIL

3 LBS. ENGLISH-CUT BEEF
SHORT RIBS (OR 2 LBS. STEW
BEEF)

1 LARGE ONION, CHOPPED

½ CUP DRY RED WINE

8 CUPS BEEF STOCK

BORSCHT

4 LARGE BEETS, PEELED AND
DICED

1 LARGE RUSSET POTATO,
PEELED AND CUT INTO
½-INCH CUBES

2 CELERY RIBS, DICED

1 SMALL RUTABAGA, PEELED
AND DICED

1 LB. CARROTS, DICED

3 TEASPOONS OLIVE OIL

½ TABLESPOON BLACK
PEPPERCORNS

½ TABLESPOON CORIANDER
SEEDS

2 SPRIGS FRESH DILL

2 SPRIGS FRESH OREGANO

2 SPRIGS FRESH ITALIAN
FLAT-LEAF PARSLEY

2 TABLESPOONS AVOCADO OIL

1 LEEK, DICED

1 LARGE ONION, DICED

2 CUPS THINLY SLICED
CABBAGE

7-OZ. CAN CHOPPED
TOMATOES AND THEIR
JUICES

½ CUP DRY RED WINE

2 TABLESPOONS RED WINE
VINEGAR

SALT, TO TASTE

FRESHLY GROUND PEPPER, TO
TASTE

DILL, FOR SERVING

GRATED HORSERADISH, FOR
SERVING

BEEF, BEET & CABBAGE BORSCHT

YIELD: **8 SERVINGS**

ACTIVE TIME: **45 MINUTES**

TOTAL TIME: **3 HOURS**

DIRECTIONS

1. Prepare the short ribs by heating oil in a large, thick-bottomed pot over medium high heat. Add the short ribs or stew beef and brown lightly on one side, then turn over.

2. Add the onions and cook for about 5 minutes. Add the wine and stock and bring to a boil. Cover and simmer, stirring occasionally, until the meat is very tender, about 2 hours. Skim off excess fat from the liquid in the pot. Remove the meat to a baking sheet, let cool, and dice. Strain the broth and reserve; discard the bones and other solids.

3. Preheat the oven to 400°F.

4. Toss the beets, potatoes, celery, rutabaga, and carrots with olive oil and spread them out in a single layer on a foil-lined roasting pan. Roast for 15 minutes.

5. Wrap the peppercorns, coriander seeds, dill, oregano, and parsley sprigs in cheesecloth and tie into a bundle.

6. In a large pot, heat the avocado oil. Add the beets, potatoes, celery, rutabaga, carrots, leek, onion, cabbage, and the herb-spice bundle. Cook, stirring occasionally, until the cabbage is wilted, about 15 minutes. Add the tomatoes and wine and simmer for about 5 minutes.

7. Stir in the strained beef broth and simmer for about 30 minutes. Stir in the vinegar and the meat and simmer for 15 minutes. Season with salt and pepper.

8. Serve the borscht with chopped dill and horseradish.

TIP:

The beauty of this soup is the shapes of the beets, carrots, and other root vegetables that shine in the bowl. This is a great way to practice knife skills, try your best to make square dice and other varieties of shapes with the root vegetables. As an alternative cooking method, try roasting beets whole on a bed of kosher salt, then peel and cut after they've cooled. This cooking method will enhance the flavors of beet and draw out moisture.

BOUILLABAISSE

DIRECTIONS

1. In a medium saucepan, warm 4 tablespoons of the olive oil over medium heat. Add the onion, leek, celery, and fennel and cook for 10 minutes, or until soft.

2. Add the garlic, bouquet garni, orange zest, and chopped tomato. Stir in the saffron and then add the fish stock, lobster stock, Pernod, and tomato paste. Season with salt and pepper and bring to a boil. Reduce heat so that the soup simmers and cook for 20 minutes.

3. Meanwhile, in a separate pan add the remaining oil and warm it over medium heat. Season the fish and shrimp with salt and pepper and cook for 2 minutes on each side. Remove both from the pan and set aside.

4. Add the clams to the broth and cook for 3 minutes. Add the mussels and cook for an additional 3 to 4 minutes. Discard any mussels that don't open.

5. Add the fish and shrimp to the broth and warm through.

6. Season with salt and pepper and ladle the soup into warm bowls. Serve with toasted baguette and Garlic Butter and garnish with parsley.

GARLIC BUTTER

1. Place the butter in a bowl and whisk for 2 minutes. Add the remaining ingredients, season with salt and pepper, and serve.

INGREDIENTS

6 TABLESPOONS EXTRA-VIRGIN
   OLIVE OIL

1 ONION, CHOPPED

1 CUP SLICED LEEK, WHITE PART
   ONLY

½ CUP SLICED CELERY

1 CUP CHOPPED FENNEL

2 GARLIC CLOVES, MINCED

BOUQUET GARNI (SEE PAGE 338)

ZEST OF 1 ORANGE

1 TOMATO, CONCASSE (SEE PAGE
   339) AND CHOPPED

PINCH OF SAFFRON

3 CUPS FISH STOCK

3 CUPS LOBSTER STOCK

2 TEASPOONS PERNOD

1 TABLESPOON TOMATO PASTE

SALT AND PEPPER, TO TASTE

1 POUND MONKFISH, CUT INTO
   1-INCH PIECES

12 SMALL SHRIMP, SHELLED AND
   DEVEINED

12 STEAMER CLAMS

24 MUSSELS

PARSLEY, CHOPPED, FOR GARNISH

TO SERVE:

BAGUETTE, SLICED AND TOASTED

GARLIC BUTTER (SEE RECIPE
   BELOW), AT ROOM TEMPERATURE

GARLIC BUTTER

1 CUP BUTTER, SOFTENED

1½ TEASPOONS LEMON JUICE

2 GARLIC CLOVES, MINCED

3 TABLESPOONS CHOPPED PARSLEY

SALT AND PEPPER, TO TASTE

BROCCOLI & CHEDDAR SOUP WITH PARMESAN CRISPS

YIELD: **4 SERVINGS**

ACTIVE TIME: **15 MINUTES**

TOTAL TIME: **30 MINUTES**

INGREDIENTS

2 TABLESPOONS EXTRA-VIRGIN OLIVE OIL

1 ONION, CHOPPED

¼ CUP BUTTER

¼ CUP FLOUR

2 CUPS MILK

2 CUPS CHICKEN STOCK

1½ CUPS BROCCOLI FLORETS

1 CUP MATCHSTICK CARROTS

2 CELERY STALKS, SLICED

2 CUPS GRATED SHARP CHEDDAR CHEESE

SALT AND PEPPER, TO TASTE

TO SERVE:

PARMESAN CRISPS

PARMESAN CRISPS

1 CUP GRATED PARMESAN CHEESE

1 CUP GRATED SHARP CHEDDAR CHEESE

CAYENNE PEPPER, TO TASTE

DIRECTIONS

1. In a medium saucepan, add the oil and warm over medium heat.

2. Add the onion and cook for 5 minutes, or until soft.

3. Add the butter. When the butter is melted, slowly add the flour, while stirring constantly. Cook for 3 minutes, and then add the milk and chicken stock.

4. Bring to a boil, reduce heat so that the soup simmers, and add the broccoli florets, carrots, and celery. Cook for 8 minutes, or until vegetables are cooked through.

5. Add cheddar cheese and mix until combined.

6. Season with salt and pepper, and serve with Parmesan Crisps.

PARMESAN CRISPS

1. Preheat the oven to 400°F.

2. In a mixing bowl, add the cheeses and mix until combined.

3. Sprinkle the cheese on a lined baking tray. Make 8 circles, using a ring cutter to help keep then round.

4. Place a pinch of cayenne on each crisp. Place the tray in the oven and cook for 7 minutes, or until melted. Let cool before serving.

BUTTERNUT SQUASH & APPLE CIDER SOUP WITH FALL SPICED CREAM

YIELD: **4 SERVINGS**

ACTIVE TIME: **30 MINUTES**

TOTAL TIME: **1 HOUR AND 20 MINUTES**

DIRECTIONS

1. In a medium saucepan, add the oil and cook over medium heat until warm. Add the onion and cook, while stirring often, for 5 minutes, or until soft.

2. Add the squash and apple. Cook, while stirring, for 5 to 10 minutes, until the squash starts to break down.

3. Add the Calvados and cook until it evaporates. Add the cider and chicken stock.

4. Bring to a boil and season with salt and pepper. Reduce heat so that the soup simmers and cook for 20 minutes, until the squash and onion are tender.

5. Transfer the soup to a food processor, puree until smooth, and strain through a fine sieve.

6. Place the soup in a clean pan and bring to a simmer. Adjust the consistency with more chicken stock if it is too thick. Adjust seasoning to taste, ladle into warm bowls, and garnish with Fall Spiced Cream, and Toasted Pumpkin Seeds.

FALL SPICED CREAM

1. In a bowl, add cream and whisk until medium peaks start to form.

2. Add the nutmeg. Season with salt and stir to combine. Refrigerate until ready to use.

TOASTED PUMPKIN SEEDS

1. Preheat the oven to 350°F.

2. Place the seeds on a baking tray and sprinkle with the olive oil and salt.

3. Place tray in oven and cook for 5 minutes. Remove, stir, and place back in the oven for another 5 minutes, until golden brown.

4. Remove from oven, set on paper towels to drain, and season to taste with salt.

INGREDIENTS

1 TABLESPOON VEGETABLE OIL

1 ONION, DICED

1 POUND BUTTERNUT SQUASH, PEELED AND DICED

1 APPLE, PEELED AND DICED

2 TABLESPOONS CALVADOS

½ CUP APPLE CIDER

2 CUPS CHICKEN STOCK

SALT AND PEPPER, TO TASTE

TO SERVE:

FALL SPICED CREAM

TOASTED PUMPKIN SEEDS

FALL SPICED CREAM

½ CUP HEAVY CREAM

½ TEASPOON NUTMEG

PINCH OF SALT

TOASTED PUMPKIN SEEDS

½ CUP RAW PUMPKIN SEEDS

½ TEASPOON EXTRA-VIRGIN OLIVE OIL

PINCH OF SALT

BUTTERNUT SQUASH & CHORIZO BISQUE

YIELD: **4 SERVINGS**

ACTIVE TIME: **15 MINUTES**

TOTAL TIME: **1 HOUR AND 30 MINUTES**

INGREDIENTS

1 LARGE BUTTERNUT SQUASH

1 ONION, QUARTERED

2 TABLESPOONS VEGETABLE OIL

SALT AND PEPPER, TO TASTE

½ LB. CHORIZO, CASING REMOVED

2 BAY LEAVES

1 CUP CREAM

1 CUP CHICKEN STOCK

1 CUP MILK

4 TABLESPOONS UNSALTED BUTTER

DIRECTIONS

1. Preheat the oven to 400°F.

2. Peel the squash, scoop out the seeds, and slice it. Toss squash and onion in oil and salt on a sheet pan and roast for 40 to 45 minutes, or until golden and fork tender. Keep an eye on the onion to make sure it doesn't burn.

3. In a pot, combine the squash and onion with the remainder of the ingredients, except the butter, and bring to a boil. Once boiling, reduce heat and simmer for 30 minutes.

4. Turn off the burner. Using an immersion blender, blend the bisque in the pot until smooth. Add butter and stir until melted and fully incorporated in the bisque.

CHICKEN NOODLE SOUP

YIELD: **4 SERVINGS**

ACTIVE TIME: **20 MINUTES**

TOTAL TIME: **30 MINUTES**

INGREDIENTS

1 TABLESPOON VEGETABLE OIL

½ ONION, FINELY CHOPPED

1 CARROT, PEELED AND FINELY CHOPPED

1 CELERY STALK, FINELY CHOPPED

1 THYME SPRIG, LEAVES REMOVED AND CHOPPED

4 CUPS CHICKEN STOCK

SALT AND PEPPER, TO TASTE

1½ CUPS MEDIUM EGG NOODLES

1 CHICKEN BREAST, SEARED AND COOKED THROUGH

DIRECTIONS

1. Place the oil in a medium saucepan and cook over medium heat until warm.

2. Add the onion and cook for 5 minutes, or until soft. Add the remaining vegetables and cook until tender.

3. Add the thyme and chicken stock and bring to a boil. Reduce heat so that the soup simmers and cook for 20 minutes.

4. Season with salt and pepper.

5. Bring to a boil again, add the egg noodles, and cook for 7 minutes, or until the noodles reach the desired tenderness.

6. Chop the seared chicken breast into ½-inch pieces and add to the soup.

7. Serve in warm bowls.

CORN AND SEAFOOD CHOWDER WITH SALT COD BEIGNETS

YIELD: **4 TO 6 SERVINGS**

ACTIVE TIME: **1 HOUR**

TOTAL TIME: **36 HOURS**

DIRECTIONS

1. In a blender, add the corn kernels and milk and puree until creamy.

2. In a medium saucepan, add the butter and cook over medium heat until melted. Add the garlic and bacon and cook for 5 minutes. Add the green-bell pepper and celery and sweat for 4 minutes, or until soft.

3. Add the rice and cook for 4 minutes. Add the flour and cook for 2 minutes, while stirring constantly.

4. Gradually add the pureed corn and stock to the saucepan. Bring to a simmer and cook for 20 minutes, or until the rice is tender.

5. Stir in the scallops, haddock, and lobster. Cook for 4 minutes and then add the parsley, cayenne pepper, and tomatoes. Cook for a few more minutes, adjust the seasoning, and ladle into warm bowls. Serve with Salt Cod Beignets and garnish with parsley.

SALT COD BEIGNETS

1. In a small saucepan, add the milk and butter and bring to a boil.

2. Add the flour, and stir until it forms a ball of dough.

3. Remove the saucepan from heat and let stand for 10 minutes.

4. Add the egg slowly and whisk until well-combined. Add the salt cod and cilantro, roll into a log, wrap with plastic wrap, and place in the freezer for 2 hours.

5. Place the oil in a Dutch oven and cook over medium-high heat until 375°F.

6. Remove the log from the freezer and cut into ½-inch thick slices.

7. Gently place each slice in the oil and fry until golden brown.

8. Use a slotted spoon to remove from oil and set on a paper towel to drain.

9. Season to taste with salt and pepper, and serve.

INGREDIENTS

1½ CUPS CORN KERNELS

2 CUPS MILK

2 TABLESPOONS BUTTER

1 GARLIC CLOVE, MINCED

4 STRIPS THICK-CUT BACON,
CHOPPED

1 GREEN BELL PEPPER, SEEDED AND
CHOPPED

¾ CUP CHOPPED CELERY

½ CUP LONG-GRAIN RICE

1 TABLESPOON ALL-PURPOSE FLOUR

2 CUPS CRAB STOCK

4 SCALLOPS, CUT INTO ¼-INCH
THICK SLICES

4 OZ. HADDOCK, CUT INTO ½-INCH
PIECES

3 OZ. LOBSTER, CUT INTO ¼-INCH
PIECES

2 TABLESPOONS CHOPPED PARSLEY,
PLUS MORE FOR GARNISH

⅛ TEASPOON CAYENNE PEPPER

1½ CUPS TOMATOES, CONCASSE
(SEE PAGE 339) AND CHOPPED

SALT AND PEPPER, TO TASTE

TO SERVE:

SALT COD BEIGNETS

SALT COD BEIGNETS

½ CUP MILK

3 TABLESPOONS BUTTER

¼ CUP ALL-PURPOSE FLOUR

1 EGG

4 OZ. SALT COD, CHOPPED

1 TABLESPOON CHOPPED CILANTRO

2 CUPS VEGETABLE OIL

INGREDIENTS

6 EARS OF CORN, KERNELS
   REMOVED, COBS RESERVED

4 OZ. BACON, CHOPPED

1 LARGE WHITE ONION, CHOPPED

3 GARLIC CLOVES, MINCED

2 LARGE POTATOES, PEELED AND
   CHOPPED

4 CUPS HEAVY CREAM

SALT AND PEPPER, TO TASTE

TO SERVE:
CORN BEIGNETS

CORN BEIGNETS

¼ CUP MILK

⅛ TEASPOON SALT

2 TABLESPOONS BUTTER

¼ CUP FLOUR

1 EGG

¼ CUP CORN

½ TEASPOON CILANTRO, CHOPPED

2 CUPS OIL

CORN CHOWDER

YIELD: **4 TO 6 SERVINGS**

ACTIVE TIME: **25 MINUTES**

TOTAL TIME: **2 HOURS AND 15 MINUTES**

DIRECTIONS

1. In a stockpot, place the reserved cobs and cover with water. Bring to a boil, reduce heat so that the stock simmers, and cook for 1 hour. Strain the stock, measure out 4 cups, and reserve.

2. In a large saucepan, add the bacon and cook over medium heat until fat renders. Add the onion and garlic and cook for 5 minutes or until soft.

3. Add the potatoes and corn kernels and cook for another 10 minutes, while stirring occasionally.

4. Add the corn stock and cook until reduced by a third.

5. Add the cream and simmer for 30 minutes. Transfer to a food processor, puree until creamy, and strain through a fine sieve.

6. Season with salt and pepper, ladle into warm bowls, and serve with Corn Beignets.

CORN BEIGNETS

1. In a medium saucepan, add milk, salt, and butter and bring to a boil.

2. Add the flour and stir constantly until a ball of dough forms.

3. Remove the pan from heat and let the dough cool for 10 minutes.

4. Add the egg to the pan and whisk vigorously.

5. Once the egg has been combined, add the corn and cilantro and stir until combined.

6. Place the oil in a Dutch oven and heat to 350°F.

7. Spoon small amounts of the batter into the hot oil and cook until golden brown.

8. Remove with a slotted spoon and set on a paper towel to drain.

9. Serve immediately.

CREAM OF BROCCOLI SOUP

YIELD: **4 SERVINGS**

ACTIVE TIME: **15 MINUTES**

TOTAL TIME: **30 MINUTES**

INGREDIENTS

2 TABLESPOONS BUTTER

1 TABLESPOON EXTRA-VIRGIN OLIVE OIL

1 ONION, DICED

1 CELERY STALK, DICED

1 CROWN OF BROCCOLI, FLORETS REMOVED AND CHOPPED

1 SPRIG THYME, LEAVES REMOVED AND CHOPPED

1 SPRIG ROSEMARY, LEAVES REMOVED AND CHOPPED

4 CUPS CHICKEN OR VEGETABLE STOCK

2 CUPS HEAVY CREAM

SALT AND PEPPER, TO TASTE

DIRECTIONS

1. In a medium saucepan, add the butter and olive oil and cook over medium heat until the butter is melted.

2. Add the onion and celery and cook for 5 minutes, or until soft.

3. Add the broccoli and herbs and cook for an additional 3 minutes.

4. Add the stock and bring to a boil.

5. Reduce the heat so that the soup simmers and cook for 5 minutes.

6. Add the heavy cream and simmer for 10 minutes, or until the broccoli is tender.

7. Remove pan from heat and transfer soup to a food processor. Puree until the soup is creamy.

8. Return the soup to a clean pan, bring to a simmer, and season with salt and pepper.

9. Serve in warmed bowls.

CREAM OF MUSHROOM WITH FUSILLI PASTA

YIELD: **4 SERVINGS**

ACTIVE TIME: **20 MINUTES**

TOTAL TIME: **45 MINUTES**

INGREDIENTS

4 TABLESPOONS UNSALTED BUTTER

1 ONION, CHOPPED

2 GARLIC CLOVES, CHOPPED

⅓ CUP MADEIRA

12 OZ. WILD MUSHROOMS

4 CUPS MUSHROOM STOCK

1½ CUPS FUSILLI PASTA

1 CUP HEAVY CREAM

SALT AND PEPPER, TO TASTE

PARSLEY, CHOPPED, FOR GARNISH

DIRECTIONS

1. In a medium saucepan, add the butter and cook over medium heat until melted. Add the onions and garlic and cook for 5 minutes, or until soft.

2. Add the Madeira and cook until it evaporates.

3. Add the mushrooms and cook until all of their moisture has been released.

4. Add the mushroom stock and bring to a boil. Reduce heat so that the soup simmers and cook for 10 minutes.

5. Transfer the soup to a food processor, puree until creamy, and then strain through a fine sieve.

6. Return the soup to a clean pan and bring to a simmer. Add the pasta and cook for 8 to 10 minutes, or until pasta is tender.

7. Add the heavy cream and simmer for 2 minutes. Season with salt and pepper and serve in warm bowls garnished with the parsley.

CREAM OF TOMATO WITH FONTINA JALAPEÑO HUSH PUPPIES

YIELD: **4 SERVINGS**

ACTIVE TIME: **30 MINUTES**

TOTAL TIME: **1 HOUR AND 15 MINUTES**

DIRECTIONS

1. Place the butter in a large saucepan and cook over medium heat until melted. Add the onion and cook for 5 minutes, or until soft.

2. Add the tomatoes, carrots, chicken stock, parsley, and thyme. Reduce heat to low and simmer for 20 minutes, or until the vegetables are tender.

3. Transfer the soup to a food processor, puree until smooth, and pass through a fine sieve.

4. Return the soup to the pan and add the cream. Reheat gently and season with salt and pepper. Ladle the soup into bowls and serve with Fontina Jalapeño Hush Puppies.

FONTINA JALAPEÑO HUSH PUPPIES

1. Place the oil in a Dutch oven and heat to 320°F.

2. Add the corn meal, flour, sugar, salt, baking powder, baking soda, and cayenne pepper to a small bowl and whisk until combined.

3. In a separate bowl, add the buttermilk, egg, and jalapeño. Whisk to combine.

4. Combine the buttermilk mixture and the dry mixture.

5. Add the cheese and stir until combined.

6. Drop spoonfuls of the batter into the hot oil and fry until golden brown.

7. Remove from oil with a slotted spoon and place on paper towels to drain.

INGREDIENTS

2 TABLESPOONS BUTTER

1 ONION, CHOPPED

2 LBS. TOMATOES, CHOPPED

2 CARROTS, PEELED AND CHOPPED

5 CUPS CHICKEN STOCK

2 TABLESPOONS CHOPPED PARSLEY
LEAVES

½ TEASPOON CHOPPED THYME
LEAVES

6 TABLESPOONS HEAVY CREAM

SALT AND PEPPER, TO TASTE

TO SERVE:

FONTINA JALAPEÑO HUSH PUPPIES

FONTINA JALAPEÑO HUSH PUPPIES

2 CUPS VEGETABLE OIL

½ CUP CORN MEAL

3 TABLESPOONS ALL-PURPOSE
FLOUR, PLUS 1½ TEASPOONS

4½ TABLESPOONS SUGAR

¾ TEASPOON SALT

¼ TEASPOON BAKING POWDER

⅛ TEASPOON BAKING SODA

⅛ TEASPOON CAYENNE PEPPER

¼ CUP BUTTERMILK

1 EGG, BEATEN

2 TABLESPOONS SEEDED AND
CHOPPED JALAPEÑO

¾ CUP GRATED FONTINA

INGREDIENTS

4 PIECES THICK-CUT BACON, CUT INTO SMALL PIECES

1 LARGE ONION, CHOPPED

4 CUPS CUBED POTATOES

4 CUPS FISH STOCK

1½ LBS. HADDOCK, SKIN REMOVED, CUT INTO ½-INCH CUBES

2 TABLESPOONS CHOPPED PARSLEY LEAVES

1 TABLESPOON CHOPPED CHIVES, PLUS MORE FOR GARNISH

1 TABLESPOON CHOPPED TARRAGON LEAVES

2 CUPS HEAVY CREAM

SALT AND PEPPER, TO TASTE

TO SERVE:

CHOWDER CRACKERS

CHOWDER CRACKERS

1 CUP ALL-PURPOSE FLOUR

1 TEASPOON SALT

1 TEASPOON SUGAR

1 TEASPOON BAKING POWDER

2 TABLESPOONS UNSALTED BUTTER, CUT INTO ¼-INCH CUBES

¼ CUP COLD WATER, PLUS 3 TABLESPOONS

CREAMY HADDOCK CHOWDER

YIELD: **4 SERVINGS**

ACTIVE TIME: **30 MINUTES**

TOTAL TIME: **1 HOUR**

DIRECTIONS

1. In a medium saucepan, add the bacon and cook over low heat until crispy.

2. Add the onion and potatoes and cook for 10 minutes.

3. Add fish stock and bring to a boil.

4. Reduce the heat so that the soup simmers and cook for 10 minutes, or until the potatoes are soft.

5. Add the haddock and the herbs and simmer for 10 minutes.

6. Add the cream and slowly return to a simmer. Season with salt and pepper, ladle into warm bowls, garnish with chives, and serve with Chowder Crackers.

CHOWDER CRACKERS

1. Preheat the oven to 375°F.

2. Add the flour, salt, sugar, and baking powder to a mixing bowl and whisk until combined. Add butter and mix with your hands until the mixture resembles a coarse meal.

3. Add the water and mix until it forms a dough. Be careful not to overmix.

4. Place the dough in a lightly floured bowl and chill in the refrigerator for 15 to 20 minutes.

5. Remove the dough from the refrigerator and place on a well-floured surface. Roll out to a ¼-inch thickness, cut dough into ½-inch diamonds, and transfer to a parchment-lined baking tray.

6. Place the tray in the oven and bake for 20 minutes, or until there is just a little color around the edges. Remove and let cool on a wire rack.

FRENCH LENTIL SOUP

YIELD: **4 TO 6 SERVINGS**

ACTIVE TIME: **25 MINUTES**

TOTAL TIME: **1 HOUR AND 15 MINUTES**

INGREDIENTS

2 TABLESPOONS VEGETABLE OIL

1 ONION, PEELED AND CHOPPED

1 GARLIC CLOVE, MINCED

1 CARROT, PEELED AND FINELY DICED

1 LEEK, WHITE PART ONLY, FINELY DICED

1 CELERY STALK, FINELY DICED

1 TABLESPOON TOMATO PASTE

1½ CUPS FRENCH LENTILS

6 CUPS CHICKEN STOCK

1 SACHET D'EPICES (SEE PAGE 340)

1 BAY LEAF

2 THYME SPRIGS, LEAVES REMOVED AND CHOPPED

¼ TEASPOON CARAWAY SEEDS

½ LEMON, SLICED

½ OZ. APPLE CIDER VINEGAR

¼ CUP RIESLING

SALT AND PEPPER, TO TASTE

TO SERVE:

CARAWAY WATER BISCUITS

CARAWAY WATER BISCUITS

½ CUP ALL-PURPOSE FLOUR

10 TABLESPOONS WATER

⅛ TEASPOON SALT

2 TABLESPOONS CARAWAY SEEDS

DIRECTIONS

1. In a medium saucepan, add the oil and warm over medium heat. Add the onion and garlic and cook for 5 minutes, or until the onion is soft.

2. Add the carrot, leek, and celery, and cook for 5 minutes, or until soft.

3. Add the tomato paste and cook, while stirring, for 2 minutes.

4. Add the lentils, stock, sachet d'epices, bay leaf, thyme, caraway seeds, and lemon slices. Bring to a boil, reduce heat so that the soup simmers, and cook for 30 minutes, or until the lentils are tender.

5. Remove the sachet d'epices and lemon slices.

6. Add the vinegar and Riesling and season with salt and pepper. Serve in warmed bowls with Caraway Water Biscuits.

CARAWAY WATER BISCUITS

1. Preheat the oven to 350°F.

2. Add the flour and water to a mixing bowl and whisk until combined. Add the salt.

3. On a parchment-lined baking tray, use a pastry brush to transfer the batter to the tray, taking care to make nice, long crackers.

4. Sprinkle with caraway seeds and place in the oven. Bake for 8 minutes, or until golden brown, then remove the tray and let crackers cool.

FRENCH ONION SOUP

YIELD: **4 SERVINGS**

ACTIVE TIME: **30 MINUTES**

TOTAL TIME: **1 HOUR AND 15 MINUTES**

INGREDIENTS

5 ONIONS, 1 HALVED, THE REMAINING 4 SLICED VERY THIN

2 TABLESPOONS VEGETABLE OIL

½ CUP SHERRY

1 TABLESPOON WORCESTERSHIRE SAUCE

2 TEASPOONS CHOPPED THYME

8 CUPS CHICKEN STOCK

SALT AND PEPPER, TO TASTE

4 SLICES OF SOURDOUGH BREAD

1½ CUPS GRATED GRUYÈRE CHEESE

DIRECTIONS

1. Place the halved onion over an open flame and char. Set aside.

2. Place the oil in a medium saucepan. Add the remaining onions and cook on the lowest heat setting for 30 minutes or until golden brown. Stir the onions every few minutes and add small amounts of water when the onions begin to stick.

3. Deglaze the pan with the sherry and Worcestershire sauce. Cook until liquid has been reduced by half.

4. Add the thyme, stock, and half-charred onion and reduce by half.

5. Meanwhile, preheat your oven's broiler.

6. Remove the half-charred onion, season the soup with salt and pepper, and pour into ceramic bowls.

7. Cover with a slice of bread and the cheese, and cook on the highest shelf to melt the cheese.

GAZPACHO

YIELD: **4 TO 6 SERVINGS**

ACTIVE TIME: **1 HOUR**

TOTAL TIME: **14 HOURS**

INGREDIENTS

4 TOMATOES, CHOPPED

½ RED ONION, PEELED AND CHOPPED

½ CUCUMBER, CHOPPED

1 RED BELL PEPPER, SEEDED AND CHOPPED

1 CELERY STALK, CHOPPED

1 CUP CHOPPED CRUSTY BREAD

2 TABLESPOONS CHOPPED PARSLEY LEAVES

2 TABLESPOONS CHOPPED CHIVES

1 GARLIC CLOVE, MINCED

¼ CUP RED WINE VINEGAR

2 TABLESPOONS EXTRA-VIRGIN OLIVE OIL

1 TEASPOON LEMON JUICE

1 TEASPOON SUGAR

2 TEASPOONS TABASCO

1 TEASPOON WORCESTERSHIRE SAUCE

2 CUPS TOMATO JUICE

SALT AND PEPPER, TO TASTE

DIRECTIONS

1. Combine all ingredients in a large bowl, cover, and place in refrigerator to marinate overnight.

2. Transfer the soup to a food processor and puree to desired consistency. Chill in refrigerator for 1 hour.

3. Adjust seasoning to taste, and serve in chilled bowls.

HAM HOCK SOUP

YIELD: **4 TO 6 SERVINGS**

ACTIVE TIME: **30 MINUTES**

TOTAL TIME: **2 HOURS AND 45 MINUTES**

INGREDIENTS

2 TABLESPOONS VEGETABLE OIL

4 HAM HOCKS

1 ONION, CHOPPED

2 CARROTS, FINELY CHOPPED

2 CELERY STALKS, FINELY CHOPPED

1 GREEN BELL PEPPER, FINELY
CHOPPED

4 THYME SPRIGS, LEAVES REMOVED
AND CHOPPED

8 CUPS HAM STOCK

2 POTATOES, PEELED AND CHOPPED
INTO ½-INCH CUBES

1 (14 OZ.) CAN STEWED TOMATOES,
CHOPPED

1 14-OZ. CAN KIDNEY BEANS

SALT AND PEPPER, TO TASTE

DIRECTIONS

1. In a large saucepan, add the oil and cook over medium-high heat until warm.

2. Add the ham hocks and cook for 5 minutes, or until evenly browned.

3. Remove the ham hocks and set aside. Add the onion, carrots, celery, green bell pepper, and thyme. Cook for 5 minutes, or until the onion is soft.

4. Return the ham hocks to the pan and add the stock.

5. Bring to a boil, reduce heat so that the soup simmers, cover, and cook for 2 hours. If necessary, add more water to make sure that the ham hocks are always covered.

6. When the meat on the ham hocks is tender and falling off the bone, remove from stock and set aside.

7. Add the potatoes and simmer for 15 minutes, or until tender.

8. Meanwhile, remove the skin and fat from the ham hocks. Remove the meat and dice.

9. Add the diced meat, tomatoes, and kidney beans to the pan and cook for 5 minutes.

10. Season with salt and pepper and serve with crusty bread.

HAM HOCK & COLLARD GREEN SOUP

YIELD: **4 SERVINGS**

ACTIVE TIME: **30 MINUTES**

TOTAL TIME: **1 HOUR AND 35 MINUTES**

INGREDIENTS

4 QUARTS WATER

1 TEASPOON SALT

1 LB. COLLARD GREENS OR KALE, CHOPPED

1 TABLESPOON VEGETABLE OIL

2 OZ. SALT PORK

½ CUP MINCED ONIONS

¼ CUP MINCED CELERY

½ CUP FLOUR

8 CUPS CHICKEN STOCK

2 SMOKED HAM HOCKS

SACHET D'EPICES (SEE PAGE 340)

½ CUP HEAVY CREAM

DIRECTIONS

1. In a medium saucepan, add the water and salt and bring to a boil. Add your greens and cook for 4 minutes, or until soft. Remove with a slotted spoon and submerge in ice water. Set aside to dry.

2. In a large saucepan, add the oil and then the salt pork. Cook over medium heat until the salt pork is melted.

3. Add the onions and celery and cook for 5 minutes, or until soft.

4. Add the flour slowly, while stirring constantly, and cook for 4 minutes.

5. Gradually add the chicken stock while whisking constantly to prevent any lumps from forming. Bring to a boil, reduce heat so that the soup simmers, and add the ham hocks and sachet d'epices. Cook for 1 hour.

6. Remove ham hocks and sachet d'epices and add the greens to the saucepan.

7. Remove meat from the ham hocks, finely dice, and return to soup.

8. Add the heavy cream, season to taste, and serve in warm bowls.

HUNGARIAN GOULASH

YIELD: **4 SERVINGS**

ACTIVE TIME: **30 MINUTES**

TOTAL TIME: **2 HOURS**

INGREDIENTS

¼ CUP FLOUR

1 LB. BEEF CHUCK ROAST, CUBED

2 TABLESPOONS VEGETABLE OIL

1 LARGE ONION, PEELED AND CHOPPED

1 GREEN BELL PEPPER, SEEDS REMOVED, CHOPPED

2 CARROTS, PEELED AND CHOPPED

1 CELERY STALK, CHOPPED

1 CUP RED WINE

2 TEASPOONS PAPRIKA

3 TABLESPOONS TOMATO PASTE

1 TEASPOON CHOPPED THYME LEAVES

1 TEASPOON CHOPPED PARSLEY LEAVES

4 CUPS BEEF STOCK

1 (14 OZ.) CAN DICED TOMATOES

1 TABLESPOON WORCESTERSHIRE SAUCE

SALT AND PEPPER, TO TASTE

¼ TEASPOON CAYENNE PEPPER

TO SERVE:
SOUR CREAM

DIRECTIONS

1. Preheat the oven to 350°F.

2. Pour the flour into a bowl and then dredge the pieces of meat in the flour until coated.

3. In a large saucepan, add the oil and cook over medium heat until warm. Add the onion, pepper, carrots, and celery and cook for 5 minutes, or until soft.

4. Add the meat and cook until browned.

5. Add the red wine and cook for 5 minutes.

6. Add the paprika, tomato paste, thyme, and parsley and cook for 2 minutes.

7. Add the stock, diced tomatoes, and Worcestershire sauce. Bring soup to a simmer, cover, and place the saucepan in the oven. Cook for 45 minutes.

8. Remove cover, stir, and cook for an additional 45 minutes, or until the steak is tender.

9. Season with salt, pepper, and cayenne pepper, ladle into bowls, and serve with sour cream and crusty bread.

IRISH COUNTRY SOUP WITH SODA BREAD

YIELD: **4 SERVINGS**

ACTIVE TIME: **30 MINUTES**

TOTAL TIME: **1 HOUR AND 15 MINUTES**

DIRECTIONS

1. In a medium saucepan, add the oil and lamb and cook over medium-high heat for 5 minutes, or until the lamb is evenly browned.

2. Add the onion, leeks, and carrots and cook for 5 minutes, or until soft.

3. Add the stock and bring to a boil. Reduce heat so that the soup simmers, and cook for 45 minutes.

4. Add the potatoes and thyme, and cook for 10 minutes, or until the potatoes are tender.

5. Remove the soup from heat and let stand for 5 minutes. Skim any fat off, strain the stock into a fresh pan, and whisk in the butter.

6. Adjust the seasoning to taste. Return the meat and vegetables back to the soup.

7. Ladle soup into warm bowls, garnish with parsley leaves, and serve with Irish soda bread.

IRISH SODA BREAD

1. Preheat the oven to 425°F.

2. Grease and flour a 9-inch round cake pan.

3. In a large bowl, combine the flour, baking soda, and salt. Gradually stir in the buttermilk until a slightly sticky ball of dough forms.

4. Place the dough onto a lightly floured surface and knead gently for a few minutes. Form the dough into a ball and then press into the prepared cake pan so that the dough resembles a large disk. The dough should reach the edges of the pan, but may spring back slightly.

5. Cut an X into the top of the dough with a sharp knife, about a ¼ inch deep. Cover the pan with another round cake pan turned upside down.

6. Place in the oven and bake for 30 minutes. Remove the top pan and bake uncovered for approximately 10 minutes, or until the crust is a dark golden brown. Remove from oven, and serve.

INGREDIENTS

1 TABLESPOON VEGETABLE OIL

1 LB. BONELESS LAMB LOIN,
TRIMMED AND CUBED

1 ONION, PEELED AND CHOPPED

2 LEEKS, WHITE PART ONLY, THINLY
SLICED

2 CARROTS, PEELED AND THICKLY
SLICED

4 CUPS VEAL STOCK

2 POTATOES, PEELED AND CUT
INTO CHUNKS

4 THYME SPRIGS, LEAVES REMOVED
AND CHOPPED

1 TABLESPOON UNSALTED BUTTER

SALT AND PEPPER, TO TASTE

PARSLEY, CHOPPED, FOR GARNISH

TO SERVE:

IRISH SODA BREAD

IRISH SODA BREAD

4 CUPS ALL-PURPOSE FLOUR

2 TEASPOONS BAKING SODA

1 TEASPOON SALT

1¾ CUPS BUTTERMILK

ITALIAN SAUSAGE SOUP

YIELD: **4 SERVINGS**

ACTIVE TIME: **20 MINUTES**

TOTAL TIME: **1 HOUR**

INGREDIENTS

2 TABLESPOONS EXTRA-VIRGIN OLIVE OIL

1 LB. HOT ITALIAN SAUSAGE

1 ONION, CHOPPED

2 CARROTS, CHOPPED

1 CELERY STALK, CHOPPED

2 GARLIC CLOVES, MINCED

6 CUPS BEEF STOCK

1 ZUCCHINI, QUARTERED, SEEDS REMOVED, CHOPPED

1 14 OZ. CAN STEWED TOMATOES

1 14 OZ. CAN CANNELLINI BEANS

2 CUPS SPINACH

SALT AND PEPPER, TO TASTE

DIRECTIONS

1. In a medium saucepan, add the olive oil and cook over medium heat until warm.

2. Add the sausage and cook for 5 minutes, or until evenly browned.

3. Use a slotted spoon to remove the sausage. Set aside.

4. Add the onion, carrots, celery, and garlic to the pan and cook for 5 minutes, or until soft.

5. Add the stock and bring to a boil. Reduce heat so that the soup simmers and cook for 10 minutes.

6. Add the zucchini, tomatoes, and beans and cook for 15 minutes.

7. Cut the cooked sausage into ¼-inch slices. Add sausage and spinach to the saucepan and simmer for 5 minutes.

8. Season with salt and pepper and serve in warm bowls.

ITALIAN WEDDING SOUP

YIELD: **4 SERVINGS**

ACTIVE TIME: **30 MINUTES**

TOTAL TIME: **1 HOUR AND 15 MINUTES**

DIRECTIONS

MEATBALLS

1. Preheat the oven to 350°F.

2. In a bowl, add all of the ingredients and mix with a fork until well combined.

3. Divide the mixture into 16 balls, roll with your hands until nice and round, and then place on a baking tray.

4. Place tray in oven and bake for 20 to 25 minutes, until nicely browned and cooked through. Remove from oven and set aside.

SOUP

1. In a medium saucepan, add the olive oil and cook over medium heat until warm. Add the onion, carrots, and celery and cook for 5 minutes, or until soft.

2. Add the stock and the wine, and bring to a boil.

3. Reduce heat so that the soup simmers, add the pasta, and cook for 8 minutes.

4. Add the cooked meatballs and simmer for 5 minutes. Add the dill and the spinach and cook for 2 minutes, or until the spinach has wilted.

5. Ladle into warm bowls and garnish with Parmesan.

INGREDIENTS

MEATBALLS

12 OZ. GROUND CHICKEN

⅓ CUP PANKO

1 GARLIC CLOVE, MINCED

2 TABLESPOONS CHOPPED PARSLEY
   LEAVES

¼ CUP GRATED PARMESAN CHEESE

1 TABLESPOON MILK

1 EGG, BEATEN

⅛ TEASPOON FENNEL SEEDS

⅛ TEASPOON RED PEPPER FLAKES

½ TEASPOON PAPRIKA

SALT AND PEPPER, TO TASTE

SOUP

2 TABLESPOONS EXTRA-VIRGIN
   OLIVE OIL

1 ONION, CHOPPED

2 CARROTS, FINELY CHOPPED

1 CELERY STALK, FINELY CHOPPED

6 CUPS CHICKEN STOCK

¼ CUP WHITE WINE

½ CUP TUBETINI PASTA

2 TABLESPOONS CHOPPED DILL

6 OZ. BABY SPINACH

SALT AND PEPPER, TO TASTE

GRATED PARMESAN CHEESE, FOR
   GARNISH

INGREDIENTS

15 STEAMER CLAMS, SCRUBBED
AND CLEANED

2 CUPS WATER

⅓ CUP CHOPPED SALT PORK

¾ CUP CHOPPED ONION

⅓ CUP DICED CARROTS

1 CUP CHOPPED LEEKS, WHITE
PART ONLY

⅓ CUP DICED GREEN BELL PEPPER

1 GARLIC CLOVE, MINCED

1 CUP TOMATO JUICE

½ CUP TOMATO, CONCASSE (SEE
PAGE 339) AND CHOPPED

1 BAY LEAF

1 SPRIG THYME

½ SPRIG OREGANO

1 CUP POTATO, PEELED AND
CHOPPED

⅛ TEASPOON TABASCO

⅛ TEASPOON WORCESTERSHIRE
SAUCE

⅛ TEASPOON OLD BAY

TO SERVE:

SALTINES

SALTINES

2 CUPS ALL-PURPOSE FLOUR

1½ TEASPOONS BAKING POWDER

2 TABLESPOONS BUTTER

¾ CUP MILK

1 EGG YOLK

1 TEASPOON WATER

COARSE SALT, TO TASTE

MANHATTAN CLAM CHOWDER WITH SALTINES

YIELD: **4 SERVINGS**

ACTIVE TIME: **45 MINUTES**

TOTAL TIME: **1 HOUR AND 30 MINUTES**

DIRECTIONS

1. In a medium saucepan, add the clams and water. Cover and cook over medium-high heat for 5 minutes, or until all the clams have opened.

2. Use a fine sieve to strain the clams from the water. Reserve the cooking liquid.

3. In a clean medium saucepan, add the salt pork and cook over medium heat until melted. Add the onion, carrots, leeks, green bell pepper, and garlic and cook for 5 minutes, or until soft.

4. Add the reserved cooking liquid, tomato juice, tomato, bay leaf, thyme, and oregano. Bring to a simmer and cook for 10 minutes.

5. Meanwhile, remove the meat from the clams. Separate the bellies and reserve. Peel the outer membrane from the clam and discard. Roughly chop the clam and set aside.

6. Add the potato to the saucepan and cook for 5 minutes, or until tender.

7. Remove the bay leaf, thyme, and oregano. Add the chopped clams and the clam bellies. Season with Tabasco, Worcestershire sauce, and Old Bay, ladle into warm bowls, and serve with Saltines.

SALTINES

1. Preheat the oven to 325°F.

2. In a mixing bowl, add the flour and baking powder and whisk until combined. Add the butter and knead with your hands until the mixture resembles a coarse meal.

3. Add the milk and mix until a dough forms. Be careful not to overmix.

4. Place the dough in a lightly floured bowl and chill in the refrigerator for 15 to 20 minutes.

5. Remove the bowl from the refrigerator and place dough on a well-floured surface. Roll out to ⅛-inch thickness. Cut dough into 2½-inch squares and transfer them to a parchment-lined baking tray.

6. Using a fork to prick holes in the squares.

7. In a small bowl, add the egg yolk and the water, and whisk until combined. Use a pastry brush to apply a very thin layer of the egg wash on each cracker.

8. Sprinkle with a small amount of coarse salt, place the tray in the oven, and bake for 20 minutes, or until there is a little color around the bottom edges. Remove and let cool on a wire rack before serving.

CHEF'S SPECIAL MATZO BALL SOUP

YIELD: **6 SERVINGS**

ACTIVE TIME: **35 MINUTES**

TOTAL TIME: **4 HOURS**

DIRECTIONS

1. In a large stockpot, place all of the soup ingredients and bring to a slow simmer with a cover on the pot. Simmer with a lazy bubble for 2 hours, until chicken is falling off the bone.

2. To make the Schmaltz balls, in a bowl, combine the eggs, Schmaltz, and sesame oil and whisk until emulsified.

3. Add the remainder of the ingredients, mix well, and refrigerate for 1 hour.

4. After 1 hour, using wet hands, make golf ball-size balls of the matzo meal.

5. Bring a large pot of salted water to a boil and cook the matzo balls for 30 minutes, covered; do not open the lid to check on the balls for any reason, just be patient and confident in your cooking.

6. When the matzo balls are fully cooked, remove them with a slotted spoon and place them in a chicken soup pot to absorb additional flavor.

7. To serve, ladle a big portion of soup, vegetables, and shredded chicken with 1 of the giant Schmaltz balls and garnish with a few sprigs of dill.

GRIBENES & SCHMALTZ

1. In a large nonstick skillet over medium heat, toss chicken skin and fat with salt and 1 tablespoon water and spread out in one layer. Cook over medium heat for about 15 minutes, until fat starts to render and skin begins to turn golden at the edges.

2. Add onion, if using, and cook 45 minutes to 1 hour, tossing occasionally, until chicken skin and onions are crispy and richly browned, but not burned.

3. Strain through a sieve. Reserve the Schmaltz and store in refrigerator for up to 6 months.

4. If you want the gribenes to be crispier, return to the skillet and cook over high heat until done to taste. Drain gribenes on a paper towel–lined plate before serving.

INGREDIENTS

SOUP

1 (4 LB.) WHOLE CHICKEN, GIBLETS REMOVED

8 QUARTS CHICKEN STOCK

1¾ TEASPOONS SEA SALT

½ CUP SCHMALTZ (SEE RECIPE))

2 LARGE SWEET WHITE ONIONS, SLICED

3 MEDIUM CARROTS, SLICED IN ¼-INCH-THICK ROUNDS

2 MEDIUM PARSNIPS, SLICED IN ¼-INCH-THICK ROUNDS

3 CELERY RIBS, DICED

1 SMALL WHITE TURNIP, PEELED AND DICED

1 SMALL YELLOW RUTABAGA, PEELED AND DICED

2 HEADS GARLIC, HALVED

½ TEASPOON FRESHLY GROUND BLACK PEPPER

1 BUNCH FLAT LEAF PARSLEY

1 BUNCH DILL

3 BAY LEAVES

1 SMALL BUNCH THYME

¼ TEASPOON GROUND TURMERIC

SCHMALTZ BALLS

2 LARGE EGGS, BEATEN

3 TABLESPOONS SCHMALTZ (SEE RECIPE)

1 TEASPOON SESAME OIL

½ CUP MATZO MEAL

½ TEASPOON BAKING POWDER

1 PINCH CINNAMON

1 TEASPOON CHOPPED FRESH DILL

½ TEASPOON DEHYDRATED GARLIC SPICE

¼ TEASPOON SEA SALT

GRIBENES & SCHMALTZ

¾ LB. CHICKEN SKIN AND FAT, DICED (USE SCISSORS, OR FREEZE THEN DICE WITH A KNIFE)

¾ TEASPOON KOSHER SALT

½ MEDIUM ONION, PEELED AND CUT INTO ¼-INCH SLICES

MENUDO

YIELD: **10 SERVINGS**

ACTIVE TIME: **30 MINUTES**

TOTAL TIME: **3 HOURS**

INGREDIENTS

3 LBS. HONEYCOMB TRIPE, CUT INTO 2- TO 3-INCH PIECES

1 LB. MARROW BONES, CUT INTO 3-INCH PIECES

SALT, TO TASTE

6 GUAJILLO CHILE PEPPERS, STEMMED AND SEEDED

2 DRIED CHILES DE ARBOL, STEMMED AND SEEDED, PLUS MORE FOR GARNISH

1 LARGE TOMATO

3 GARLIC CLOVES

1 TABLESPOON DRIED MEXICAN OREGANO, PLUS MORE FOR GARNISH

1 TEASPOON CUMIN

5 CUPS HOMINY

WHITE ONION, CHOPPED, FOR GARNISH

½ CUP CHOPPED CILANTRO, FOR GARNISH

CORN TORTILLAS, WARM, FOR SERVING

LIME WEDGES, FOR SERVING

DIRECTIONS

1. Place the tripe and marrow bones in a large saucepan and fill it with water. Bring to a boil, season generously with salt, and reduce the heat to low. Cook for 2½ hours.

2. Place the chiles in a bowl. Pour 2 cups of the warm broth over the chiles and let them soak for 20 minutes.

3. Place the chilies, soaking liquid, tomato, and garlic in a blender and puree until smooth. Strain the sauce into the saucepan, stir in the oregano and cumin, and add the hominy, if using. Continue to cook over low heat.

4. When the flavor has developed to your liking and the tripe is very tender, ladle the soup into warmed bowls and garnish with the chopped onion, cilantro, and additional arbol chile and oregano. Serve with warm tortillas and lime wedges.

MULLIGATAWNY CHICKEN CURRY SOUP WITH CURRIED CASHEWS

YIELD: **4 SERVINGS**

ACTIVE TIME: **20 MINUTES**

TOTAL TIME: **45 MINUTES**

INGREDIENTS

1 ONION, CHOPPED

2 CARROTS, PEELED AND CHOPPED

2 CELERY STALKS, CHOPPED

¼ CUP UNSALTED BUTTER

2 TABLESPOONS ALL-PURPOSE FLOUR

1 TABLESPOON CURRY POWDER

1 TABLESPOON POPPY SEEDS

1 TEASPOON CUMIN

4 CUPS CHICKEN STOCK

⅓ CUP LONG-GRAIN RICE

1 APPLE, PEELED, CORED, AND CHOPPED

1 CUP COOKED AND CHOPPED DARK CHICKEN MEAT

¼ TEASPOON DRIED THYME

½ CUP HEAVY CREAM

SALT AND PEPPER, TO TASTE

CILANTRO, FOR GARNISH

TO SERVE:

CURRIED CASHEWS

CURRIED CASHEWS

2 TABLESPOONS UNSALTED BUTTER

½ CUP UNSALTED RAW CASHEWS

1 TEASPOON CURRY POWDER

SALT, TO TASTE

DIRECTIONS

1. In a large stockpot, add the onion, carrots, celery, and butter and cook over medium heat for 5 minutes, or until soft.

2. Stir in the flour, curry powder, poppy seeds, and cumin and cook for 3 minutes. Pour in the chicken stock and bring to a boil.

3. Add the rice, reduce heat so that the soup simmers, and cook for 15 minutes.

4. Add in the apple, chicken, and thyme and simmer for 10 more minutes.

5. Add the cream, return to a simmer, season with salt and pepper, garnish with cilantro, and serve with Curried Cashews.

CURRIED CASHEWS

1. In a small sauté pan, add the butter and cook over medium heat until melted.

2. Add the cashews and cook for 4 minutes, while stirring constantly.

3. Add the curry powder and cook until the cashews are golden brown.

4. Remove, set on a paper towel, season with salt, and reserve until ready to serve.

OAXACAN BLACK BEAN SOUP

YIELD: **4 TO 6 SERVINGS**

ACTIVE TIME: **30 MINUTES**

TOTAL TIME: **1 HOUR AND 30 MINUTES**

INGREDIENTS

10 CUPS WATER

1½ CUPS DRIED BLACK BEANS, RINSED

½ CUP FENNEL, CHOPPED

½ CUP CHOPPED ANDOUILLE SAUSAGE

1 ONION, CHOPPED

2 CUPS VEGETABLE OIL

6 CORN TORTILLAS, CUT INTO ⅛-INCH STRIPS

24 MEDIUM SHRIMP, PEELED AND CLEANED

CILANTRO, CHOPPED, FOR GARNISH

QUESO FRESCO OR FETA, FOR GARNISH

8 OZ. CRAB MEAT, COOKED

DIRECTIONS

1. Combine the water and beans in a large saucepan and bring to a simmer. Add the fennel, sausage, and onion and cook for approximately 1 hour, until the beans are tender.

2. Transfer the soup to a food processor and puree to a fine consistency, adding more water if necessary.

3. Return the soup to a clean pan and bring to a simmer.

4. Meanwhile in a small saucepan, add the oil and cook over medium-high heat until it is 350°F. Add the tortilla strips, turning frequently until they are crisp. Remove with a slotted spoon and set on paper towels to drain.

5. Once the soup is simmering, add the shrimp and crab and cook for 4 minutes, or until the shrimp are cooked.

6. Ladle into warmed bowls and garnish with cheese, tortilla crisps, and cilantro.

OLD FASHIONED CHICKEN BROTH & DUMPLING SOUP

YIELD: **4 SERVINGS**

ACTIVE TIME: **30 MINUTES**

TOTAL TIME: **1 HOUR AND 15 MINUTES**

INGREDIENTS

BROTH

1 TABLESPOON VEGETABLE OIL

½ ONION, FINELY CHOPPED

1 CARROT, PEELED AND FINELY CHOPPED

1 CELERY STALK, FINELY CHOPPED

1 THYME SPRIG, LEAVES REMOVED AND CHOPPED

4 CUPS CHICKEN STOCK

SALT AND PEPPER, TO TASTE

PARSLEY, CHOPPED, FOR GARNISH

CHICKEN DUMPLINGS

4 SLICES OF BREAD, CHOPPED

½ CUP CHOPPED PARSLEY LEAVES

1¼ CUPS ALL-PURPOSE FLOUR

1 TEASPOON BAKING POWDER

½ CUP MILK

1 EGG

¼ CUP UNSALTED BUTTER, MELTED

1 CUP COOKED AND CHOPPED DARK CHICKEN MEAT

SALT AND PEPPER, TO TASTE

4 CUPS CHICKEN STOCK

DIRECTIONS

BROTH

1. Add the oil to a medium saucepan and warm over medium heat. Add the onions and cook for 5 minutes, or until soft. Add the remaining vegetables and cook until tender.

2. Add the thyme and the chicken stock and bring to a boil. Reduce the heat so that the soup simmers and cook for 20 minutes.

3. Season with salt and pepper, ladle into bowls with the chicken dumplings, and garnish with parsley.

CHICKEN DUMPLINGS

1. Place the bread and parsley in a food processor and pulse until combined. Add the flour and the baking powder, pulse, then slowly add the milk, egg, and butter. Pulse until a smooth paste forms and transfer to a mixing bowl.

2. Fold in the chopped chicken meat and season with salt and pepper. Refrigerate for 1 hour.

3. Drop tablespoon-sized balls into the simmering broth. Cover and cook for 12 minutes.

YIELD: **4 SERVINGS**

ACTIVE TIME: **15 MINUTES**

TOTAL TIME: **30 MINUTES**

PASTA FAGIOLI

INGREDIENTS

2 TABLESPOONS EXTRA-VIRGIN OLIVE OIL

1 ONION, PEELED AND CHOPPED

2 CARROTS, PEELED AND GRATED

2 CELERY STALKS, CHOPPED

1 GARLIC CLOVE, MINCED

4 CUPS CHICKEN STOCK

1 (14 OZ.) CAN OF STEWED TOMATOES, CHOPPED

2 TABLESPOONS MEDITERRANEAN HERBS (SEE RECIPE)

1 CUP ELBOW PASTA

1 (14 OZ.) CAN OF PINTO BEANS

SALT AND PEPPER, TO TASTE

1 CUP SHAVED PARMESAN CHEESE, FOR GARNISH

MEDITERRANEAN HERBS

1 TABLESPOON DRIED ROSEMARY

2 TEASPOONS CUMIN

2 TEASPOONS GROUND CORIANDER

1 TEASPOON DRIED OREGANO

⅛ TEASPOON SALT

DIRECTIONS

1. In a medium saucepan, add oil and cook over medium heat.

2. When oil is warm, add onion, carrots, celery, and garlic and cook for 5 minutes, or until soft.

3. Add the stock, tomatoes, and Mediterranean Herbs and bring to a boil.

4. Reduce heat so that soup simmers, add elbow pasta, and cook for 10 minutes.

5. Add the pinto beans and cook for an additional 5 minutes.

6. Season with salt and pepper, garnish with Parmesan cheese, and serve in warmed bowls.

MEDITERRANEAN HERBS

1. Mix all the ingredients together in a small bowl and then store in an airtight container until ready to use.

POZOLE

YIELD: **8 SERVINGS**

ACTIVE TIME: **30 MINUTES**

TOTAL TIME: **14 HOURS AND 15 MINUTES**

INGREDIENTS

2 TABLESPOONS EXTRA-VIRGIN
   OLIVE OIL

2 LBS. BONELESS PORK SHOULDER,
   CUBED

1 LARGE YELLOW ONION, CHOPPED

SALT AND PEPPER, TO TASTE

4 DRIED CHIPOTLE PEPPERS,
   STEMMED, SEEDED, AND
   CHOPPED

2 CUPS HOMINY

1 TABLESPOON FRESH THYME

2 TABLESPOONS CUMIN

3 GARLIC CLOVES, MINCED

CILANTRO, CHOPPED, FOR
   GARNISH

LIME WEDGES, FOR SERVING

DIRECTIONS

1. Coat the bottom of a Dutch oven with the olive oil and warm it over medium-high heat. Add the pork and onion, season with salt and pepper, and cook, stirring occasionally, until pork and onion are well browned, about 10 minutes.

2. Add the chipotles and hominy, cover the mixture with water, and add the thyme and cumin. Bring the soup to a boil, reduce the heat so that it simmers, and cook until the pork and hominy are very tender, about 1½ hours, stirring occasionally.

3. Add the garlic, cook for 5 minutes, and taste the soup. Adjust the seasoning as necessary, ladle the soup into warmed bowls, garnish with cilantro, and serve with lime wedges.

INGREDIENTS

4 POUNDS STEAMER CLAMS

2 CUPS WHITE WINE

2 CUPS CHOPPED ONIONS

4 TABLESPOONS UNSALTED BUTTER

1 TEASPOON CHOPPED THYME
  LEAVES

2 CUPS YUKON GOLD POTATOES

4 CUPS HEAVY CREAM

SALT AND PEPPER, TO TASTE

PARSLEY, CHOPPED, FOR GARNISH

TO SERVE:

OYSTER CRACKERS

OYSTER CRACKERS

1 CUP ALL-PURPOSE FLOUR

1 TEASPOON SALT

1 TEASPOON SUGAR

1 TEASPOON BAKING POWDER

2 TABLESPOONS UNSALTED
  BUTTER, CUT INTO ¼-INCH
  CUBES

¼ CUP COLD WATER, PLUS 3
  TABLESPOONS

NEW ENGLAND CLAM CHOWDER

YIELD: **4 TO 6 SERVINGS**

ACTIVE TIME: **45 MINUTES**

TOTAL TIME: **1 HOUR AND 30 MINUTES**

DIRECTIONS

1. In a medium saucepan add the clams, wine, and half of the chopped onions. Cover and cook over medium-high heat for 5 minutes, or until all the clams have opened.

2. Strain through a fine sieve. Set the clams aside and reserve the cooking liquid.

3. In a clean medium saucepan, add the butter and cook over medium heat until melted. Add the remaining onions and cook for 5 minutes, or until soft.

4. Add the reserved cooking liquid and thyme and bring to a simmer. Cook for 5 minutes, or until the liquid has been reduced by half.

5. Meanwhile, remove the meat from the clams. Separate the bellies and reserve. Peel the outer membrane from the clam and discard. Roughly chop the clam.

6. Add the potatoes and heavy cream to the saucepan and cook for 5 minutes, or until the potatoes are tender.

7. Add the chopped clams and clam bellies. Season with salt and pepper, and ladle into warm bowls. Garnish with parsley and serve with Oyster Crackers.

OYSTER CRACKERS

1. Preheat the oven to 375°F.

2. Add the flour, salt, sugar, and baking powder to a mixing bowl and whisk until combined. Add the butter and mix with your hands until the mixture resembles a coarse meal.

3. Add the water and mix until a dough forms. Be careful not to overmix.

4. Place the dough in a lightly floured bowl and chill in the refrigerator for 15 to 20 minutes.

5. Remove the bowl from the refrigerator and place on a well-floured surface. Roll to a ¼-inch thickness, cut into small circles with a ring cutter, and transfer to a parchment-lined baking tray.

6. Bake for 20 minutes, or until there is a little color around the bottom edges of the crackers. Remove and let cool on a wire rack before serving.

PHO

YIELD: **4 SERVINGS**

ACTIVE TIME: **30 MINUTES**

TOTAL TIME: **3 HOURS AND 50 MINUTES**

INGREDIENTS

2 LBS. BEEF OR CHICKEN BONES

1 SMALL YELLOW ONION, HALVED

1-INCH PIECE OF GINGER, UNPEELED

2 CINNAMON STICKS

3 STAR ANISE

2 CARDAMOM PODS, SEEDS REMOVED AND CHOPPED

1 TABLESPOON BLACK PEPPERCORNS

5 CLOVES

1 TABLESPOON CORIANDER SEED

1 TABLESPOON FENNEL SEED

1 CUP CILANTRO, LEAVES AND STEMS

8 CUPS WATER

1 TABLESPOON FISH SAUCE

1 TABLESPOON HOISIN

BLACK PEPPER, TO TASTE

1 TEASPOON SRIRACHA

3 OZ. RICE NOODLES

JALAPEÑO, SLICED, FOR GARNISH

BEAN SPROUTS, FOR GARNISH

LIME WEDGES, FOR GARNISH

THAI BASIL, FOR GARNISH

DIRECTIONS

1. Preheat the oven to 350°F.

2. Place the bones in the oven and roast for 20 minutes, or until golden brown.

3. Meanwhile, over an open flame, char your onion and ginger.

4. Place all of the spices in a nonstick pan and cook over medium heat for 2 to 3 minutes, until they become nice and fragrant.

5. Add the bones, the charred onion and ginger, spices, cilantro and the water in a large saucepan and bring to a boil.

6. Reduce heat so that the soup simmers and cook for 3 hours.

7. Strain the soup into a fresh clean pot. Season with fish sauce, hoisin, black pepper, and Sriracha. Return to a simmer.

8. Place the rice noodles into a bowl and cover with boiling water. Let soak for 4 minutes, or according to manufacturer's instructions.

9. Place the rice noodles into warm bowls. Ladle the soup over the noodles and garnish with sliced jalapeño, bean sprouts, lime wedges, and Thai basil.

INGREDIENTS

1 TABLESPOON SESAME OIL

1 ONION, FINELY CHOPPED

2 CARROTS, FINELY CHOPPED

2 GARLIC CLOVES, FINELY CHOPPED

1 CUP SAKE

4 CUPS CHICKEN STOCK

1 LEMONGRASS STALK, BRUISED
WITH THE BACK OF A KNIFE

1 TABLESPOON SOY SAUCE

1 TABLESPOON FISH SAUCE

12 WONTONS

SALT AND PEPPER, TO TASTE

SHALLOTS, SLICED, FOR GARNISH

BEAN SPROUTS, FOR GARNISH

CILANTRO, CHOPPED, FOR
GARNISH

PORK AND SHRIMP WONTONS

4 OZ. SHRIMP, PEELED AND
DEVEINED, FINELY CHOPPED

8 OZ. GROUND PORK

1 TABLESPOON SHALLOTS, MINCED

1 TABLESPOON CHIVES, CHOPPED

1 TABLESPOON FISH SAUCE

2 TABLESPOONS MISO

1 TABLESPOON SHRIMP PASTE

2 TABLESPOONS CHOPPED RADISH

1 TABLESPOON SESAME SEEDS,
TOASTED

1 TEASPOON SESAME OIL

1 TEASPOON SHERRY

12 WONTON WRAPPERS

PORK & SHRIMP WONTON SOUP

YIELD: **4 SERVINGS**

ACTIVE TIME: **40 MINUTES**

TOTAL TIME: **1 HOUR**

DIRECTIONS

1. In a medium saucepan, add the sesame oil and cook over medium heat until warm. Add the onion and carrots and cook for 5 minutes, or until soft.

2. Add the garlic and cook for 2 minutes. Add the sake, chicken stock, lemongrass, soy sauce, and fish sauce, simmer for 10 minutes, and then remove the lemongrass.

3. Bring the soup to a boil and add the wontons. Reduce the heat so that the soup simmers and cook for 5 minutes, or until the wontons float to the top. Season with salt and pepper.

4. Place 3 wontons in each bowl, pour the soup over the top of the wontons, and garnish with the shallots, bean sprouts, and cilantro.

PORK AND SHRIMP WONTONS

1. Combine all ingredients in a bowl, except the wonton wrappers, and mix until well combined.

2. Place 2 teaspoons of the mixture in the center of a wonton wrapper.

3. Dip your finger into cold water and rub it around the entire edge of the wonton. Bring each corner of the wrapper together and seal together. Repeat with remaining wonton wrappers and refrigerate until ready to use.

SEAFOOD & SAUSAGE GUMBO

YIELD: **4 TO 6 SERVINGS**

ACTIVE TIME: **30 MINUTES**

TOTAL TIME: **1 HOUR**

DIRECTIONS

1. To make a roux, heat the oil in a medium saucepan. Once the oil is hot, add the flour a little at a time and blend until it is a smooth paste.

2. Cook for about 5 to 10 minutes, while stirring constantly, until the roux is the color of peanut butter. Remove pan from heat and set aside to cool.

3. In a medium saucepan, add the butter and cook over medium heat until melted. Add the onion, peppers, and celery. Cook for 5 minutes, or until the onions have softened.

4. Add the sausage and garlic and cook for 5 minutes.

5. Add the bay leaf, thyme, and cayenne. Stir in the stock, tomatoes, and okra. Bring to a boil, reduce heat so that the soup simmers, and cook for 10 minutes.

6. Meanwhile, cook the rice according to the manufacturer's instructions.

7. Whisk the roux into the soup and return to a boil, while whisking constantly. Lower the heat and simmer for 5 minutes.

8. Add the shrimp, crab, and calamari. Cook for 3 to 4 minutes, or until the shrimp turns pink and the calamari bodies begin to curl.

9. Season with salt, pepper, and, if using, the Tabasco.

10. To serve, put a scoop of rice in the middle of a warm bowl and ladle the gumbo around it.

SCORING CALAMARI

Separate the squid's body from the tentacles. Cut the body in half and separate the two halves. Flip them over so that the skin is right-side up and gently cut crisscross patterns into them with a sharp knife, being careful not to cut into the flesh

INGREDIENTS

½ CUP VEGETABLE OIL

½ CUP ALL-PURPOSE FLOUR

4 TABLESPOONS UNSALTED BUTTER

1 ONION, FINELY CHOPPED

1 CUP CHOPPED GREEN BELL
PEPPER

1 CUP CHOPPED RED BELL PEPPER

2 CELERY STALKS, CHOPPED

1 LB. ANDOUILLE SAUSAGE, CUT
INTO ½-INCH SLICES

2 GARLIC CLOVES, MINCED

1 BAY LEAF

¼ TEASPOON CHOPPED THYME
LEAVES

½ TEASPOON CAYENNE PEPPER

3 CUPS LOBSTER OR CRAB STOCK

1 CUP TOMATO, CONCASSE (SEE
PAGE 339) AND CHOPPED

1 CUP CANNED, CUT OKRA

1½ CUPS LONG-GRAIN RICE

1½ LBS. RAW SHRIMP, PEELED AND
DEVEINED

8 OZ. CRAB MEAT, COOKED AND
CLEANED

8 OZ. CALAMARI, TENTACLES
WHOLE, BODIES HALVED AND
SCORED

SALT AND PEPPER, TO TASTE

TABASCO, TO TASTE

INGREDIENTS

SWEDISH MEATBALLS

1 CUP PANKO

½ CUP HEAVY CREAM

2 TABLESPOONS EXTRA-VIRGIN
OLIVE OIL

1 ONION, CHOPPED

8 OZ. GROUND BEEF

8 OZ. GROUND PORK

1 EGG

⅛ TEASPOON ALLSPICE

SALT AND PEPPER, TO TASTE

SOUP

¼ CUP BUTTER

2 CARROTS, PEELED AND CHOPPED

2 CELERY STALKS, CHOPPED

2 CUPS THINLY SLICED BUTTON
   MUSHROOMS

2 GARLIC CLOVES, MINCED

⅓ CUP FLOUR

6 CUPS BEEF STOCK

¾ CUP HEAVY CREAM

1 TEASPOON WORCESTERSHIRE
   SAUCE

½ TEASPOON PAPRIKA

½ TEASPOON RED PEPPER FLAKES

SALT AND PEPPER, TO TASTE

PARSLEY, CHOPPED, FOR GARNISH

SWEDISH MEATBALL SOUP

YIELD: **4 TO 6 SERVINGS**

ACTIVE TIME: **30 MINUTES**

TOTAL TIME: **1 HOUR AND 15 MINUTES**

DIRECTIONS

SWEDISH MEATBALLS

1. In a mixing bowl, add the bread crumbs and cream. Let bread soak for 10 minutes.

2. In a small sauté pan, add 1 tablespoon of the oil and warm over medium heat. Add the onion and cook for 5 minutes, or until soft. Turn off the heat and let onion cool.

3. Once cool, add the cooked onion to the mixing bowl. Add the remaining ingredients and stir until well combined.

4. Place a small amount of the mixture in the microwave or cook a small amount on the stove. Taste and adjust seasoning accordingly.

5. Divide the mixture into 24 piles and roll each one into a nice, round ball.

6. In a large saucepan, add the remaining oil and cook over medium-high heat until warm.

7. Add the meatballs to the pan and cook for 5 minutes, while stirring constantly. When they are golden brown all over, remove and set aside.

SOUP

1. In a large saucepan, add the butter and cook over medium heat until warm.

2. Add the carrots and celery and cook for 3 minutes. Add the mushrooms and garlic and cook for 3 more minutes, or until the celery and carrots are soft.

3. Add the flour and cook for 3 minutes. Slowly add the beef stock to the pan, stirring constantly to prevent any lumps from forming.

4. Bring to a boil. Reduce heat so that the soup simmers, add the Swedish Meatballs, and cook for 15 minutes, or until meatballs are cooked through.

5. Add the cream, Worcestershire sauce, paprika, and red pepper flakes. Cook for 5 minutes, season with salt and pepper, ladle into bowls, and garnish with parsley.

SIMPLE DUMPLING SOUP

YIELD: **4 SERVINGS**

ACTIVE TIME: **30 MINUTES**

TOTAL TIME: **1 HOUR**

INGREDIENTS

DUMPLINGS

1 CUP ALL-PURPOSE FLOUR

½ TEASPOON BAKING POWDER

½ TEASPOON SALT

½ TABLESPOON EXTRA-VIRGIN
OLIVE OIL

1 EGG

6 TABLESPOONS WATER

1 TABLESPOON CHOPPED CHIVES

SOUP

2 TABLESPOONS UNSALTED BUTTER

4 SLICES THICK-CUT BACON,
CHOPPED

1 ONION, CHOPPED

4 CUPS PEELED AND CHOPPED
POTATOES

6 CUPS CHICKEN STOCK

SALT AND PEPPER, TO TASTE

DIRECTIONS

DUMPLINGS

1. Add the flour, baking powder, and salt to a mixing bowl and stir until combined.

2. Add the oil, egg, water, and chives and stir with a fork until a loose dough forms. Cover dough and set aside.

SOUP

1. In a medium saucepan, add the butter and cook over medium heat until warm.

2. Add the bacon and onion and cook for 5 minutes, or until the bacon is crispy and the onion is soft.

3. Add the potatoes and cook for 3 minutes. Add the stock and bring to a boil.

4. Reduce heat so that the soup simmers and cook for 10 minutes, or until the potatoes are tender.

5. Season with salt and pepper. Drop tablespoon-sized dumplings into the broth.

6. Once all of the dumplings have been incorporated, simmer for 3 minutes then turn off the heat.

7. Let stand a few minutes, then ladle into warmed bowls and serve.

YIELD: **4 TO 6 SERVINGS**

ACTIVE TIME: **20 MINUTES**

TOTAL TIME: **45 MINUTES**

TOM KHA KAI

INGREDIENTS

2 CUPS SLICED SHIITAKE MUSHROOMS

2 (14 OZ.) CANS OF COCONUT MILK

4 SCALLIONS, WHITE PART ONLY, SLICED

4-INCH LEMONGRASS STALK, BRUISED WITH THE BACK OF A KNIFE

1-INCH PIECE OF GALANGAL ROOT

1 SMALL RED CHILI PEPPER, SEEDS REMOVED, FINELY DICED

1 LIME LEAF

2 TEASPOONS GRATED GINGER

½ CUP FISH SAUCE, OR TO TASTE

JUICE OF 2 LIMES

1 LB. CHICKEN BREAST, CUT INTO 1-INCH CUBES

1 TEASPOON SUGAR

BEAN SPROUTS, FOR GARNISH

DIRECTIONS

1. Rinse, dry, and remove the stems from the mushrooms.

2. In a medium saucepan, add the coconut milk and bring to a simmer over medium heat.

3. Add the mushrooms, scallions, lemongrass, galangal root, red chili pepper, lime leaf, and ginger. Cook, while lightly stirring, for about 5 minutes, until the contents of the pan are fragrant.

4. Add fish sauce, lime juice, chicken breast, and sugar. Raise heat to medium-high and cook for 10 minutes, or until the chicken is cooked through.

5. Remove the lemongrass and galangal, ladle into warm bowls, and garnish with bean sprouts.

TOMATO SOUP WITH CHEDDAR CHEESE DUMPLINGS

YIELD: **4 SERVINGS**

ACTIVE TIME: **30 MINUTES**

TOTAL TIME: **1 HOUR**

INGREDIENTS

2 TABLESPOONS UNSALTED BUTTER

1 ONION, CHOPPED

5 CUPS CHICKEN STOCK

2 CARROTS, PEELED AND CHOPPED

2 LBS. TOMATOES, CHOPPED

2 TABLESPOONS CHOPPED PARSLEY LEAVES, PLUS MORE FOR GARNISH

½ TEASPOON CHOPPED THYME LEAVES

6 TABLESPOONS HEAVY CREAM, PLUS MORE FOR GARNISH

SALT AND PEPPER, TO TASTE

PARMESAN CHEESE, SHAVED, FOR GARNISH

CHEDDAR CHEESE DUMPLINGS

¾ CUP ALL-PURPOSE FLOUR

1 TEASPOON BAKING POWDER

¼ TEASPOON SALT

⅓ CUP GRATED SHARP CHEDDAR CHEESE

½ CUP BUTTERMILK

3 TABLESPOONS CHOPPED PARSLEY LEAVES

DIRECTIONS

1. Place the butter in a large saucepan and cook over medium heat until melted.

2. Add the onion and cook for 5 minutes, or until soft.

3. Stir in the tomatoes, carrots, chicken stock, parsley, and thyme, reduce to low, and simmer for 20 minutes, or until the vegetables are tender.

4. Transfer the soup to a food processor, puree, and then pass through a fine sieve.

5. Return the soup to the pan and add the cream. Reheat gently, season with salt and pepper, and let simmer while you prepare the Cheddar Cheese Dumplings.

CHEDDAR CHEESE DUMPLINGS

1. Combine the flour, baking powder, and salt in a mixing bowl. Add the cheddar cheese, buttermilk, and parsley, and mix with a fork until a dough forms.

2. When the dough becomes thick, use your hands and knead it until it is nice and smooth. Add water or flour, as necessary.

3. Drop tablespoon-sized dumplings into the simmering tomato soup.

4. Once all the dough has been incorporated, simmer for 10 minutes. Turn off heat and let stand for a few minutes. Ladle into warm bowls, and garnish with Parmesan, a splash of heavy cream, and parsley.

INGREDIENTS

4 TABLESPOONS UNSALTED BUTTER

6 LEEKS, WHITE PART ONLY, THINLY
   SLICED

3 LARGE SHALLOTS, CHOPPED

1 IDAHO POTATO, PEELED AND
   CUBED

6 CUPS CHICKEN STOCK

SALT AND PEPPER, TO TASTE

PINCH OF NUTMEG

1 CUP HEAVY CREAM

TO SERVE:

CHIVE OIL

SIMPLE CROUTONS

CHIVE OIL

1 CUP CHOPPED CHIVES

1 CUP BABY SPINACH

1 CUP VEGETABLE OIL

SIMPLE CROUTONS

SLICED BRIOCHE, CUT INTO
   ¼-INCH CUBES

1 TABLESPOON EXTRA-VIRGIN
   OLIVE OIL

SALT AND PEPPER, TO TASTE

VICHYSSOISE

YIELD: **4 SERVINGS**

ACTIVE TIME: **40 MINUTES**

TOTAL TIME: **2 HOURS**

DIRECTIONS

1. In a medium saucepan, add the butter and cook over medium heat until warm. Add the leeks and shallots and cook for 5 minutes, or until soft.

2. Add the potato and cook for 3 minutes.

3. Add the chicken stock and bring to a boil. Reduce to a simmer, partially cover the pan, and cook until potato is soft.

4. Transfer to a food processor, puree until creamy, and strain through a fine sieve.

5. Season with salt, pepper, and nutmeg. Add the heavy cream and place the soup in the refrigerator to chill.

6. Serve in chilled bowls with Chive Oil and Simple Croutons.

CHIVE OIL

1. In a small saucepan, bring 4 cups of water to boil.

2. Add the chives and spinach, cook for 1 minute, remove, and submerge in ice water.

3. Remove from ice water and squeeze out any excess water.

4. In a food processor, add the chives, spinach, and the oil. Puree for 3 to 4 minutes, strain through cheesecloth, and reserve until ready to use.

SIMPLE CROUTONS

1. Preheat the oven to 350°F.

2. Spread the brioche out on a baking tray.

3. Drizzle with olive oil and bake for 5 minutes, or until golden brown.

4. Remove, season with salt and pepper, and place on a paper towel to cool.

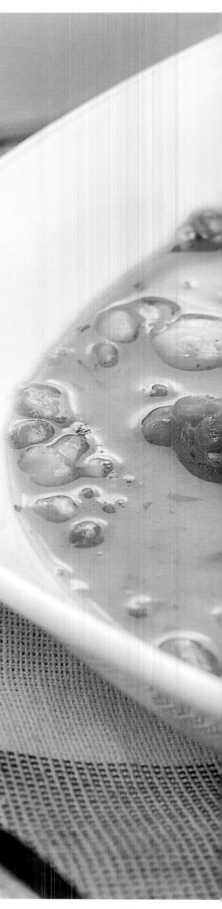

CHAPTER 3

GLOBAL FLAVORS

Taste your way around the world with these recipes that feature an exciting range of bold spices, nuanced umami, and creamy decadence.

YIELD: **6 SERVINGS**

ACTIVE TIME: **25 MINUTES**

TOTAL TIME: **50 MINUTES**

ALBONDIGAS SOUP

INGREDIENTS

2 LBS. GROUND BEEF

1 EGG

2 TABLESPOONS COOKED RICE

3 SPRIGS FRESH HIERBABUENA, FINELY CHOPPED, PLUS MORE TO TASTE

2 SPRIGS FRESH OREGANO, FINELY CHOPPED

½ BUNCH FRESH PARSLEY, FINELY CHOPPED

SALT, TO TASTE

4 LARGE TOMATOES

¼ ONION

2 GARLIC CLOVES

1 TEASPOON CUMIN

½ TEASPOON TOMATO PASTE

2 TABLESPOONS EXTRA-VIRGIN OLIVE OIL

3 CARROTS, PEELED AND SLICED

3 ZUCCHINI, SLICED

CORN TORTILLAS, WARM, FOR SERVING

ROASTED SERRANO OR JALAPEÑO CHILIE PEPPERS, FOR SERVING

DIRECTIONS

1. In a large mixing bowl, combine the ground beef, egg, rice, hierbabuena, oregano, and parsley and season the mixture with salt. Form the mixture into meatballs that weigh about 1 ounce a piece.

2. Place the tomatoes, onion, and garlic in a small saucepan, add water, and boil until the vegetables are tender. Drain, add the vegetables to a blender with the cumin and tomato paste, and puree until smooth.

3. Place the oil in a large saucepan and warm over medium heat. Add the puree and cook for 2 minutes.

4. Add 4 cups of water and season with salt. If desired, add more sprigs of hierbabuena to the broth. Bring to a simmer.

5. Add the carrots and meatballs and cook over low heat until the meatballs are completely cooked through, about 20 minutes.

6. Add the zucchini and cook until tender, about 5 minutes.

7. Ladle the soup into warmed bowls and serve with warm tortillas and roasted chilies.

AVIKAS

INGREDIENTS

1 TABLESPOON OLIVE OIL

1 LB. CHUCK BEEF, CHOPPED INTO 2-INCH CUBES

3 TEASPOONS SEA SALT, DIVIDED

1 YELLOW ONION, ROUGHLY CHOPPED

1 TABLESPOON TOMATO PASTE

½ CUP WHITE KIDNEY BEANS, SOAKED OVERNIGHT AND DRAINED

¼ TEASPOON GROUND BLACK PEPPER

WHITE RICE, TO SERVE

DIRECTIONS

1. Add the oil to a large pot over medium-high heat.

2. Season the meat with 1 teaspoon salt. Once the oil is hot, place the pieces of meat into the pot and sear on all sides until deep golden brown, about 3 minutes on each side. Transfer the meat to a plate.

3. Add the onions to the pot and sauté until golden, about 10 minutes, scraping the meat drippings on the bottom of the pot to incorporate. Add the tomato paste and cook for about 2 minutes until caramelized. Add the meat back into the pot, along with the beans, pepper, and remaining salt. Cover with water and stir.

4. Bring the mixture to a boil and reduce to a gentle simmer. Add a lid slightly ajar and continue cooking the stew for about 1 hour and 30 minutes, until the mixture cooks down into a stew-like consistency and the beans and meat are tender.

5. Serve hot with white rice.

BAKED POTATO SOUP

YIELD: **4 SERVINGS**

ACTIVE TIME: **20 MINUTES**

TOTAL TIME: **1 HOUR AND 30 MINUTES**

INGREDIENTS

2 LARGE IDAHO POTATOES

¼ CUP UNSALTED BUTTER

⅓ CUP ALL-PURPOSE FLOUR

4 CUPS MILK

1½ CUPS GRATED SHARP CHEDDAR CHEESE

½ CUP SOUR CREAM

SALT AND PEPPER, TO TASTE

⅔ CUP CHOPPED SCALLIONS, FOR GARNISH

8 SLICES THICK-CUT BACON, COOKED AND CHOPPED, FOR GARNISH

DIRECTIONS

1. Preheat the oven to 400°F.

2. Use a fork to pierce the potatoes. Place them on a baking tray and bake for 1 hour, or until tender.

3. When potatoes are cooked, remove from oven and allow them to cool slightly. Peel and mash with a fork.

4. Meanwhile, in a medium saucepan add the butter and cook over medium heat until it is melted.

5. Add the flour and stir until combined.

6. Add the milk and bring soup to a simmer, while stirring constantly. Cook for 5 minutes, or until the soup thickens.

7. Add the mashed potatoes and half of the cheese. Stir until the cheese melts.

8. Remove the pan from heat and stir in the sour cream.

9. Season with salt and pepper and serve in bowls garnished with scallions and bacon.

BARLEY, DILL & PORK SOUP

YIELD: **4 TO 6 SERVINGS**

ACTIVE TIME: **20 MINUTES**

TOTAL TIME: **2 HOURS**

INGREDIENTS

1 TABLESPOON VEGETABLE OIL

1¾ LBS. PORK SHOULDER, CUT
  INTO ½-INCH PIECES

1 ONION, CHOPPED

2 CELERY STALKS, CHOPPED

2 CARROTS, PEELED AND CHOPPED

¼ CUP PERNOD

1 GARLIC CLOVE, MINCED

2 SPRIGS THYME, LEAVES REMOVED
  AND CHOPPED

8 CUPS BEEF OR VEAL STOCK

8 OZ. PEARL BARLEY

½ CUP CHOPPED DILL

SALT AND PEPPER, TO TASTE

DIRECTIONS

1. In a large saucepan, add the oil and cook over medium-high heat until warm. Add the pork and cook, while turning, for 5 minutes, or until evenly browned. Remove with a slotted spoon and set aside.

2. Add the onion, celery, and carrots, and cook for 5 minutes, or until soft.

3. Add the Pernod, garlic, and thyme and cook until the Pernod has been reduced by half.

4. Return the pork to the saucepan. Add the stock and the barley and bring to a boil.

5. Reduce heat so that the soup simmers. Cover and cook over low heat for 1 hour and 30 minutes, or until pork is very tender.

6. Add the dill, season with salt and pepper, and serve in warm bowls.

YIELD: **6 SERVINGS**

ACTIVE TIME: **30 MINUTES**

TOTAL TIME: **2 HOURS AND 20 MINUTES**

INGREDIENTS

2 LBS. RED CABBAGE, CORE REMOVED, SHREDDED

2 ONIONS, PEELED AND FINELY SLICED

1 LARGE APPLE, PEELED, CORED, AND CHOPPED

3 TABLESPOONS BROWN SUGAR

2 GARLIC CLOVES, MINCED

¼ TEASPOON GRATED NUTMEG

½ TEASPOON CARAWAY SEEDS

3 TABLESPOONS APPLE CIDER VINEGAR

4 CUPS VEAL STOCK

SALT AND PEPPER, TO TASTE

2 TABLESPOONS EXTRA-VIRGIN OLIVE OIL

1½ LBS. SIRLOIN STEAK, FAT REMOVED

WATERCRESS, FOR GARNISH

TO SERVE:

HORSERADISH CREAM

HORSERADISH CREAM

2 PEELED AND GRATED FRESH HORSERADISH

2 TEASPOONS WHITE WINE VINEGAR

½ TEASPOON DIJON MUSTARD

1 CUP HEAVY CREAM

SALT AND PEPPER, TO TASTE

BEEF AND BRAISED CABBAGE SOUP WITH HORSERADISH CREAM

DIRECTIONS

1. Preheat the oven to 300°F.

2. In a mixing bowl, add the cabbage, onions, apple, brown sugar, garlic, nutmeg, caraway seeds, and vinegar with a ½ cup of the stock. Mix until well combined.

3. Season with salt and pepper and transfer to a large, buttered casserole dish. Cover the pan and place it in the oven. Cook for 1 hour and 30 minutes, removing to stir the contents of the casserole dish.

4. Turn off the oven and open the oven door slightly.

5. When the dish has cooled slightly, remove it from the oven and set aside. Preheat the oven to 450°F.

6. In a medium sauté pan, add the olive oil and warm over medium heat. Season the sirloin with salt and pepper and then add to pan. Cook until golden brown on both sides. Remove sirloin from the pan and set aside.

7. Spoon the cabbage dish into a large saucepan. Add the remaining stock and bring to a boil. Reduce heat so that the soup simmers.

8. Place the sirloin in the oven and cook until it is the desired level of doneness.

9. Remove the sirloin from the oven and let it stand for 5 minutes. Ladle the soup into serving bowls. Thinly slice the steak and place it on top of the soup. Serve with Horseradish Cream and watercress.

HORSERADISH CREAM

1. Combine the horseradish, vinegar, mustard, and 4 tablespoons of the cream in a mixing bowl.

2. Lightly whip the remaining cream and then fold this into the horseradish mixture. Season to taste and refrigerate until ready to serve.

BEEF, BARLEY & PORTOBELLO MUSHROOM SOUP

YIELD: **4 TO 6 SERVINGS**

ACTIVE TIME: **20 MINUTES**

TOTAL TIME: **2 HOURS**

INGREDIENTS

1 TABLESPOON VEGETABLE OIL

1¾ LBS. BEEF STEW MEAT, CUT INTO 1-INCH PIECES

1 ONION, CHOPPED

2 CELERY STALKS, CHOPPED

2 CARROTS, PEELED AND CHOPPED

½ CUP RED WINE

1 GARLIC CLOVE, MINCED

2 SPRIGS THYME, LEAVES REMOVED AND CHOPPED

8 CUPS BEEF OR VEAL STOCK

¾ CUP PEARL BARLEY

1 LB. PORTOBELLO MUSHROOMS, SLICED

SALT AND PEPPER, TO TASTE

DIRECTIONS

1. In a large saucepan, warm oil on medium-high heat.

2. Add the beef and cook for 5 minutes, or until evenly browned, then remove with a slotted spoon and reserve.

3. Add the onion, celery, and carrots and cook for 5 minutes or until soft.

4. Add the red wine, garlic, and thyme and reduce by half.

5. Add the seared beef, the stock, and the barley and bring to a boil.

6. Reduce to a simmer, cover, and cook on low heat for 1 hour and 30 minutes.

7. Add the mushrooms and cook for 10 minutes or until the beef is very tender.

8. Season with salt and pepper and serve in warmed bowls.

BOULETTES WITH CHICKEN & VEGETABLE SOUP & COUSCOUS

YIELD: **6 SERVINGS**

ACTIVE TIME: **1 HOUR**

TOTAL TIME: **2 HOURS AND 30 MINUTES**

INGREDIENTS

BOULETTES

1 YELLOW ONION, ROUGHLY CHOPPED

1 CUP ROUGHLY CHOPPED CILANTRO OR PARSLEY

1½ LBS. GROUND BEEF

½ CUP BREAD CRUMBS

3 TEASPOONS SEA SALT

1 TEASPOON FRESHLY GROUND BLACK PEPPER

6 EGGS

2 CUPS ALL-PURPOSE FLOUR

1 TABLESPOON WATER

AVOCADO OIL, FOR FRYING

SAUCE

3 TABLESPOONS CANOLA OIL

1 YELLOW ONION, FINELY CHOPPED

1 TABLESPOON TOMATO PASTE

1 CUP WATER

1 TEASPOON SEA SALT

SOUP

3 TABLESPOONS AVOCADO OIL

6 CHICKEN DRUMSTICKS OR 4 CHICKEN BREASTS, SKIN ON AND BONE IN

1 YELLOW ONION, FINELY CHOPPED

2 TEASPOONS GROUND CORIANDER

3 TEASPOONS GROUND CUMIN

2 TEASPOONS SEA SALT

½ TEASPOON FRESHLY GROUND BLACK PEPPER

6 WHOLE CLOVES, DIVIDED

2 TABLESPOONS TOMATO PASTE

½ CUP OF WATER

4 CARROTS, CHOPPED

3 SMALL TURNIPS, CHOPPED

2 CUPS CHOPPED BUTTERNUT SQUASH

4 SMALL YUKON GOLD POTATOES, PEELED AND CHOPPED

1 YELLOW ONION

7 EGGS

½ CUP MINCED CILANTRO

3 ZUCCHINI, PEELED AND CHOPPED

6 HEARTS OF CANNED ARTICHOKES

2 CUPS CANNED CHICKPEAS, RINSED AND DRAINED

COUSCOUS

8 OZ. COUSCOUS

1 TABLESPOON AVOCADO OIL

1 TEASPOON SEA SALT

WARM WATER

1 TEASPOON HARISSA, FOR GARNISH (OPTIONAL)

DIRECTIONS

1. Place the onion and cilantro in a food processor and process until a smooth paste is formed, about 5 minutes. Transfer the paste into a large bowl. Add the beef, breadcrumbs, salt, pepper, and 3 eggs. Mix well until all of the ingredients are evenly incorporated into the meatball mixture.

2. Take about 1½ tablespoons of the mixture and shape it into an oval meatball. Place it onto a platter and continue shaping the remaining mixture into meatballs. Set aside.

3. To make the sauce, add oil to a wide and deep pan over medium-high heat. Add the onion and sauté for about 8 to 10 minutes, until browned. Add the tomato paste, 1 cup water, and salt and mix well. Reduce the heat to medium-low and simmer for about 3 minutes, until the tomato paste dissolves. Remove from heat and set aside.

4. To continue making the boulettes, place 2 cups flour in a wide and shallow bowl. Crack 3 eggs into another wide and shallow bowl and add 1 tablespoon water to the eggs. Beat the eggs well. Set aside.

5. Add about ¾ inch of oil to a wide and deep saucepan over medium-high heat. While the oil is heating up, start dredging the meatballs.

6. Take one meatball and gently place it into the bowl with flour, rolling it to cover all the edges with flour. Shake off any excess flour. Dip the floured meatball into the beaten eggs and roll the meatball so all the edges are covered with the egg. Shake off any excess egg from the meatball. Repeat until all of the meatballs have been dredged.

7. Once the oil is sizzling in the pan, gently place the dredged meatballs in the oil, making sure not to overcrowd the pan. Fry the meatballs on each side until golden brown, about 3 to 5 minutes per side. Transfer the fried meatballs to a paper towel–lined plate and fry the remaining meatballs.

8. Gently place the fried meatballs into the pan with the sauce that was set aside. Add enough water to just cover the meatballs three-quarters of the way up.

9. Place the pan over medium-high heat and simmer until the water has reduced by half and the meatballs are cooked through, about 15 minutes. Set aside.

10. To prepare the soup, place 3 tablespoons of oil in a large pot over medium heat. Once the oil is sizzling, add the chicken in one layer and sprinkle the onions around the meat. Sear the chicken on both sides until golden brown, about 5 minutes per side. Stir the onions occasionally until they are softened and lightly browned.

11. Meanwhile, in a bowl, combine the coriander, cumin, salt, pepper, 2 cloves, tomato paste, and ½ cup water and mix well.

12. Once the chicken is seared on both sides, add the spice and tomato paste mixture to the pot. Stir the chicken and onions in the sauce and cook for about 3 minutes. Reduce the heat to medium and add the carrots, turnips, squash, and potatoes.

13. Peel the whole onion, press 4 garlic cloves into the onion's surface, and add it into the pot.

14. Gently place the eggs, in their shells, in the pot over the vegetables. Add enough water to cover the eggs, chicken, and vegetables. Cook over a simmer, uncovered, for 30 minutes.

15. Add the zucchini, artichokes, and chickpeas and continue cooking for another 15 to 20 minutes, until the chicken, vegetables, and eggs are cooked through.

16. Transfer the eggs from the pot and remove their shells. Place the peeled eggs back into the soup and set the soup aside.

17. Place the couscous in a large heatproof bowl or baking dish. Add enough boiling water to just cover the couscous and let it sit for 10 to 15 minutes, or until tender. Once the couscous is ready use a fork to gently fluff and mix it.

18. To serve, place a small mound of couscous on each plate and top with a boulette, a piece of chicken, an egg, and some vegetables. If desired, add harissa for some spice. Serve hot.

BROKEN PASTA SOUP

YIELD: **4 SERVINGS**

ACTIVE TIME: **20 MINUTES**

TOTAL TIME: **45 MINUTES**

INGREDIENTS

2 TEASPOONS EXTRA-VIRGIN OLIVE OIL

1 ONION, CHOPPED

2 GARLIC CLOVES, MINCED

2 CARROTS, PEELED AND CHOPPED

1 ZUCCHINI, SEEDS REMOVED AND CHOPPED

4 CELERY STALKS, CHOPPED

2 (14 OZ.) CANS STEWED TOMATOES

4 CUPS VEGETABLE STOCK

2 OZ. SPAGHETTI, BROKEN INTO 2-INCH PIECES

2 TABLESPOONS PARSLEY, LEAVES REMOVED AND CHOPPED

SALT AND PEPPER, TO TASTE

TO SERVE:

PESTO

DIRECTIONS

1. In a medium saucepan, add the oil and cook over medium heat until warm. Add the onion and cook for 5 minutes, or until soft. Add the garlic, carrots, zucchini, and celery, and cook for 5 minutes. Add the tomatoes and stock, and bring to a boil.

2. Reduce heat so that the soup simmers and cook for 15 minutes.

3. Add the spaghetti and cook for 8 to 10 minutes, or until the pasta is tender.

4. Stir in the parsley, season with salt and pepper, and serve in warm bowls with pesto.

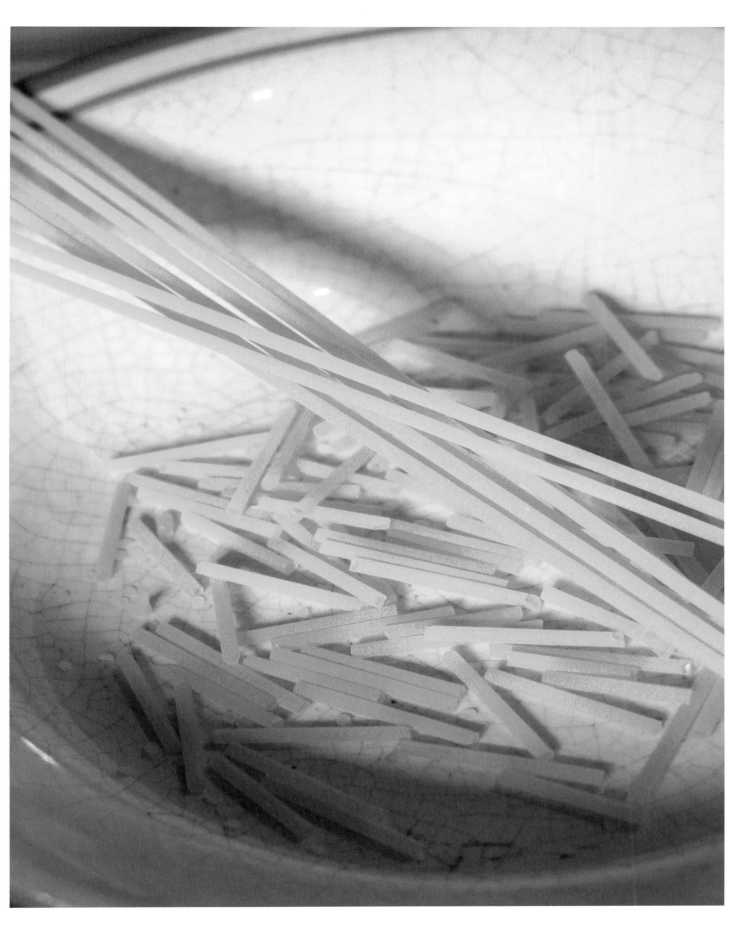

BULGARIAN SOUR LAMB SOUP WITH PAPRIKA BUTTER

YIELD: **4 SERVINGS**

ACTIVE TIME: **25 MINUTES**

TOTAL TIME: **1 HOUR AND 35 MINUTES**

INGREDIENTS

2 TABLESPOONS VEGETABLE OIL

1 LB. LAMB SHOULDER, TRIMMED AND CUBED

1 ONION, PEELED AND DICED

2 TABLESPOONS ALL-PURPOSE FLOUR

1 TABLESPOON PAPRIKA

4 CUPS LAMB OR VEAL STOCK

3 SPRIGS FRESH PARSLEY

4 SCALLIONS

4 SPRIGS FRESH DILL, PLUS MORE FOR GARNISH

¼ CUP LONG-GRAIN RICE

2 EGGS, BEATEN

2–3 TABLESPOONS DISTILLED VINEGAR

SALT AND PEPPER, TO TASTE

TO SERVE:

PAPRIKA BUTTER

PAPRIKA BUTTER

4 TABLESPOONS UNSALTED BUTTER, SOFTENED

2 TEASPOONS PAPRIKA

DIRECTIONS

1. In a medium saucepan, add the oil and cook over medium heat until warm. Add the lamb and cook for 5 minutes, or until brown on all sides.

2. Add the onion and cook 5 minutes, or until soft.

3. Sprinkle in the flour and the paprika and cook for 2 minutes. Add the stock, while stirring vigorously, and let soup simmer for 10 minutes.

4. Tie the parsley, scallions, and dill together and add to the soup.

5. Add the rice, bring to a boil, and reduce the heat so that the soup simmers. Cook for 30 to 40 minutes, or until the lamb is tender.

6. Remove the pan from heat and stir in the eggs.

7. Add the vinegar, discard the bunch of herbs, and season to taste.

8. Serve in a warmed bowl. Place a coin of Paprika Butter on top, allow it to melt, and then garnish with the dill.

PAPRIKA BUTTER

1. In a bowl, add the butter and paprika and whisk together. Quenelle the butter and roll it into logs in plastic wrap.

2. Chill until ready to serve.

BUTTERNUT SQUASH, QUINOA, AND CHICKEN SOUP

YIELD: **4 SERVINGS**

ACTIVE TIME: **20 MINUTES**

TOTAL TIME: **1 HOUR AND 15 MINUTES**

INGREDIENTS

1 BUTTERNUT SQUASH, HALVED AND SEEDED

3 TABLESPOONS EXTRA-VIRGIN OLIVE OIL

2 CHICKEN BREASTS, CUT INTO ½ INCH CUBES

1 ONION, CHOPPED

2 GARLIC CLOVES, MINCED

4 CUPS CHICKEN STOCK

1 (14 OZ.) CAN CHOPPED STEWED TOMATOES

1 OREGANO SPRIG, LEAVES REMOVED AND CHOPPED

⅔ CUP QUINOA

SALT AND PEPPER, TO TASTE

DIRECTIONS

1. Preheat the oven to 375°F.

2. Place butternut squash on baking tray, sprinkle with oil, and place in oven flesh side down for 30 minutes, or until the flesh is very tender.

3. Meanwhile, in a heavy-bottom pan, warm the remaining oil over medium heat.

4. Add the chicken breast and cook for 5 minutes, or until evenly browned. Remove with a slotted spoon, and set aside.

5. Add the onion and cook for 5 minutes or until soft.

6. Add the garlic and cook for an additional 2 minutes.

7. Add 3 cups of the stock, stewed tomatoes, and oregano and bring to a boil, then reduce to a simmer.

8. Scoop the cooked flesh from the baked butternut squash, add to a food processor with the remaining chicken stock, and puree.

9. Add the butternut squash puree, chicken, and quinoa to the simmering broth and simmer for 15 minutes or until the quinoa is tender.

10. Season with salt and pepper and serve in warmed bowls.

CHICKEN & CORN SUCCOTASH SOUP

YIELD: **4 SERVINGS**

ACTIVE TIME: **20 MINUTES**

TOTAL TIME: **1 HOUR**

INGREDIENTS

¼ CUP UNSALTED BUTTER

4 SLICES OF THICK-CUT BACON, CUT INTO ¼-INCH PIECES

2 ONIONS, CHOPPED

2 GARLIC CLOVES, MINCED

2 CHICKEN BREASTS, SKIN REMOVED AND CHOPPED INTO ½-INCH PIECES

¼ CUP ALL-PURPOSE FLOUR

4 CUPS CHICKEN STOCK

4 EARS OF CORN, KERNELS REMOVED

1 (14 OZ.) CAN KIDNEY BEANS, RINSED AND DRAINED

1 CUP HEAVY CREAM

3 TABLESPOONS CHOPPED PARSLEY LEAVES

SALT AND PEPPER, TO TASTE

DIRECTIONS

1. In a medium saucepan, add the butter and cook over medium heat until melted. Add the bacon, onions, and garlic and cook for 5 minutes. Add the chicken breasts and cook for 5 minutes.

2. Add the flour and cook, while stirring constantly, for 5 minutes.

3. Add the chicken stock slowly, whisking constantly to prevent lumps from forming.

4. Bring to a boil. Reduce heat so that the soup simmers. Add the corn kernels and kidney beans and simmer for 5 minutes.

5. Add the cream and return to a simmer. Add chopped parsley, season with salt and pepper, and serve in warm bowls.

CHICKEN PARM SOUP

YIELD: **4 SERVINGS**

ACTIVE TIME: **20 MINUTES**

TOTAL TIME: **1 HOUR**

INGREDIENTS

2 TABLESPOONS EXTRA-VIRGIN OLIVE OIL

2 CHICKEN BREASTS, CUT INTO ½-INCH PIECES

1 ONION, CHOPPED

2 GARLIC CLOVES, MINCED

1 TEASPOON CRUSHED RED PEPPER FLAKES

¼ CUP TOMATO PASTE

1 (14 OZ.) CAN DICED STEWED TOMATOES

6 CUPS CHICKEN STOCK

2 CUPS PENNE PASTA

2 CUPS GRATED PARMESAN CHEESE

1 CUP GRATED MOZZARELLA CHEESE, PLUS MORE FOR GARNISH

SALT AND PEPPER, TO TASTE

BASIL, CHOPPED, FOR GARNISH

DIRECTIONS

1. In a medium saucepan, add the oil and warm over medium-high heat. Add the chicken and cook for 5 minutes, while turning, until golden brown.

2. Add the onion and garlic and cook for 5 minutes, or until the onion is soft.

3. Add the red pepper flakes, tomato paste, tomatoes, and stock, and bring to a boil.

4. Reduce heat so that the soup simmers and cook for 10 minutes.

5. Add the penne and cook for 12 minutes. Add the mozzarella and Parmesan and stir until they melt. Season with salt and pepper, ladle into bowls, and garnish with basil and Parmesan.

CHICKEN TORTILLA SOUP

YIELD: **4 TO 6 SERVINGS**

ACTIVE TIME: **30 MINUTES**

TOTAL TIME: **1 HOUR AND 30 MINUTES**

INGREDIENTS

8 CORN TORTILLAS

3 TABLESPOONS CANOLA OIL

2 TABLESPOONS KOSHER SALT, PLUS MORE FOR SEASONING

2 TABLESPOONS MINCED GARLIC

6 BONELESS, SKINLESS CHICKEN THIGHS

½ LARGE YELLOW ONION, DICED

1 POBLANO PEPPER, SEEDED AND DICED

1 ANAHEIM PEPPER, SEEDED AND DICED

4 PLUM TOMATOES, DICED

2 TABLESPOONS ADOBO SAUCE FROM A CAN OF CHIPOTLES IN ADOBO

1 TABLESPOON CUMIN

2 DRIED ARBOL CHILES, SEEDED AND MINCED

4 CUPS CHICKEN STOCK

1 CUP WATER

COTIJA CHEESE, FOR GARNISH

CILANTRO, CHOPPED, FOR GARNISH

DIRECTIONS

1. Preheat the oven to 375°F. Cut 6 of the tortillas into small strips and set 2 aside.

2. Line a baking sheet with parchment paper and place the tortilla strips on the sheet. Brush the strips with 1 tablespoon of the oil and then sprinkle them with kosher salt. Place the sheet in the oven and bake for 15 to 20 minutes, or until they become crispy. Remove from the oven and set aside.

3. Place the remaining oil and the garlic in the Dutch oven and cook over medium-high heat until the oil and garlic become fragrant, about 5 minutes.

4. Add the chicken to the pot and sear for 5 minutes on each side. Remove the chicken from the pot and set aside. The chicken should still be slightly undercooked.

5. Place the onion, peppers, tomatoes, adobo sauce, cumin, and chiles in the pot and cook for 10 to 15 minutes, stirring the mixture every couple of minutes.

6. Return the chicken to the pan. Add the 2 tablespoons of kosher salt, chicken stock, and water and cook for 1 hour or until the chicken shreds easily when pressed against the side of the pot with a wooden spoon.

7. Add the reserved whole tortillas and continue cooking until they dissolve, about 10 minutes. Garnish with Cotija cheese, cilantro, and your crispy tortilla strips.

CHICKPEA & PASTA SOUP

YIELD: **4 SERVINGS**

ACTIVE TIME: **15 MINUTES**

TOTAL TIME: **14 HOURS AND 30 MINUTES**

INGREDIENTS

1¼ CUP DRIED CHICKPEAS, SOAKED OVERNIGHT

1 TABLESPOON DRIED KOMBU

3 GARLIC CLOVES

2 TABLESPOONS EXTRA-VIRGIN OLIVE OIL, PLUS MORE FOR GARNISH

2 ROSEMARY SPRIGS, 1 LEFT WHOLE, LEAVES REMOVED AND CHOPPED FROM THE OTHER

1 CUP DITALINI PASTA

SALT AND PEPPER, TO TASTE, PLUS MORE PEPPER FOR GARNISH

DIRECTIONS

1. Rinse the chickpeas and then place in a medium saucepan. Cover with 6 cups of water, add the kombu and the cloves of garlic, and bring to a simmer. Cook for 2 hours, or until the chickpeas are nice and tender.

2. Reserve ¼ of the cooked chickpeas. Transfer the remaining contents of the saucepan to a food processor and puree.

3. In a medium heavy-bottom pan, add the olive oil and warm over medium-high heat.

4. Gently place the whole rosemary sprig into the pan and cook for a few minutes, until it is soft and fragrant. Remove the rosemary sprig and discard. Add the chickpea puree and reserved chickpeas. Add the pasta and cook for 10 minutes. If the soup becomes too thick, add more water.

5. Add the chopped rosemary, season with salt and pepper , and ladle into warm bowls. Garnish with a splash of olive oil and black pepper, and serve with crusty bread.

CHILI TORTILLA SOUP

YIELD: **4 SERVINGS**

ACTIVE TIME: **25 MINUTES**

TOTAL TIME: **1 HOUR AND 15 MINUTES**

INGREDIENTS

2 GARLIC CLOVES, UNPEELED

1 TOMATO

2 CUPS VEGETABLE OIL, PLUS 1 TABLESPOON

1 ONION, SLICED

1½ OZ. DRIED PASILLA CHILES, STEMMED AND SEEDED, SOAKED IN HOT WATER FOR 20 MINUTES AND THEN DRAINED

6 CUPS CHICKEN STOCK

8 CORN TORTILLAS, CUT INTO ¼-INCH STRIPS

4 CUPS RED SWISS CHARD

2 CUPS GRATED MONTEREY JACK CHEESE, FOR GARNISH

1 SMALL LIME, CUT INTO QUARTERS, FOR GARNISH

DIRECTIONS

1. Preheat the oven to 350°F.

2. Place the garlic in an ungreased, nonstick pan. Cook over medium heat for 15 minutes, or until blackened, turning occasionally. Remove the garlic from the pan and allow to cool. When cool, peel and mince.

3. Place the tomato on a baking tray. Place the tray in the oven and cook for 10 minutes. Remove and set aside, making sure to save any juices.

4. In a medium saucepan, add 1 tablespoon of vegetable oil and warm over low heat. Add the onion and cook for 10 minutes, or until golden brown.

5. Place the rehydrated chiles in a food processor with the roasted garlic, tomato, the tomato's juices, and 1 cup of the stock. Puree until smooth, strain though a fine sieve, and add to the cooked onions.

6. Add the remaining stock and simmer for 30 minutes.

7. Meanwhile, place the remaining 2 cups of oil in a Dutch oven and warm to 350°F. Place the tortilla strips in the oil and fry, turning frequently, until crisp. Remove with a slotted spoon and set on paper towels to drain.

8. After 30 minutes, add the red Swiss chard to the soup and cook for 5 minutes.

9. Ladle into bowls and serve with the tortilla strips, Monterey Jack cheese, and limes.

CHILLED PEANUT BUTTER AND JELLY SOUP

YIELD: **4 CHILD-SIZED SERVINGS**

ACTIVE TIME: **15 MINUTES**

TOTAL TIME: **1 HOUR AND 15 MINUTES**

INGREDIENTS

PEANUT SOUP

2 TABLESPOONS UNSALTED BUTTER

1 CELERY STALK, CHOPPED

½ ONION, CHOPPED

1 TABLESPOON ALL-PURPOSE FLOUR

2 CUPS CHICKEN STOCK

½ CUP MILK

½ CUP PEANUT BUTTER

STRAWBERRY SOUP

2 CUPS STRAWBERRIES, GREENS
    REMOVED AND CHOPPED

1½ CUPS GREEK YOGURT

JUICE OF 1 LIME

1 TEASPOON SALT

1 CUP POWDERED SUGAR, SIEVED

¼ CUP HEAVY CREAM

DIRECTIONS

PEANUT SOUP

1. In a small saucepan, add the butter and cook over medium heat until it is melted. Add the celery and onions and cook for 3 minutes, or until soft.

2. Add the flour and cook for 2 minutes.

3. Slowly add the chicken stock and milk to the pan. Let soup simmer for 5 minutes, or until it has thickened.

4. Transfer the soup to a food processor and blend until smooth.

5. Return to the pan and add the peanut butter. Whisk until combined and then chill in the refrigerator for 1 hour.

STRAWBERRY SOUP

1. Combine all ingredients in a food processor and puree until smooth. Place in the refrigerator and chill for 1 hour.

CRAB & OYSTER GUMBO

YIELD: **4 TO 6 SERVINGS**

ACTIVE TIME: **30 MINUTES**

TOTAL TIME: **1 HOUR**

INGREDIENTS

⅓ CUP VEGETABLE OIL

½ CUP ALL-PURPOSE FLOUR

½ CUP GREEN BELL PEPPER, CHOPPED

½ CUP RED BELL PEPPER, CHOPPED

1 ONION, CHOPPED

1 CELERY STALK, CHOPPED

1 GARLIC CLOVE, MINCED

4 OZ. ANDOUILLE SAUSAGE, CUT IN ⅛-INCH SLICES

3 CUPS CRAB STOCK

2 CUPS LOBSTER STOCK

¾ CUP ORZO

30 OYSTERS, SHUCKED AND RINSED, LIQUID RESERVED

½ LB. CRAB MEAT, CLEANED AND COOKED

4 SCALLIONS, WHITE PART CHOPPED, GREENS RESERVED FOR GARNISH

1 TEASPOON TABASCO

SALT AND PEPPER, TO TASTE

DIRECTIONS

1. To make a Cajun roux: In a medium saucepan, add the oil and warm over medium heat. Add the flour and whisk vigorously until combined. Cook, while stirring constantly, for 8 minutes, or until the roux resembles peanut butter.

2. Add the bell peppers, onion, celery, garlic, and sausage and cook for 4 minutes. Add the stock 1 cup at a time, while stirring constantly. Bring to a boil, reduce heat so that the soup simmers, and cook for 10 minutes. Add the orzo and simmer for an additional 10 minutes.

3. Add the oysters and their reserved liquid, the crab meat, and the scallions. Cook for 3 minutes, add the Tabasco, salt, and pepper, and then serve in warm bowls garnished with the scallion greens.

INGREDIENTS

TURKEY STOCK

1 LEFTOVER TURKEY CARCASS

4 QUARTS WATER

2 CELERY STALKS, CHOPPED

2 CARROTS, PEELED AND CHOPPED

1 ONION, CHOPPED

2 THYME SPRIGS

2 BAY LEAVES

6 BLACK PEPPERCORNS

CREAMED VEGETABLE SOUP

2 TABLESPOONS VEGETABLE OIL

1 ONION, CHOPPED

2 CELERY STALKS, CHOPPED

1 CELERIAC, PEELED AND CHOPPED

2 PARSNIPS, PEELED AND CHOPPED

1 ROSEMARY SPRIG, LEAVES
   REMOVED AND CHOPPED

½ CUP WHITE WINE

4 CUPS TURKEY STOCK

1 CUP HEAVY CREAM

SALT AND PEPPER, TO TASTE

TO SERVE:

TURKEY DUMPLINGS

TURKEY DUMPLINGS

4 SLICES OF BREAD, CHOPPED

½ CUP PARSLEY, LEAVES REMOVED
   AND CHOPPED

1¼ CUPS ALL-PURPOSE FLOUR

1 TEASPOON BAKING POWDER

½ CUP MILK

1 EGG

¼ CUP BUTTER, MELTED

1 CUP COOKED TURKEY LEG MEAT,
   CHOPPED

SALT AND PEPPER, TO TASTE

4 CUPS TURKEY STOCK

CREAMED VEGETABLE SOUP WITH TURKEY DUMPLINGS

YIELD: **4 SERVINGS**

ACTIVE TIME: **45 MINUTES**

TOTAL TIME: **4 HOURS AND 15 MINUTES**

DIRECTIONS

TURKEY STOCK

1. Place all of the ingredients in a large stockpot. Bring to a boil, reduce heat so that stock simmers, and cook for 3½ hours, or until nice and flavorful.

2. Skim top to remove impurities from the stock. Strain through a fine sieve and set aside.

CREAMED VEGETABLE SOUP

1. In a medium saucepan, warm the oil over medium heat. Add the onion, celery, celeriac, and parsnips and cook for 10 minutes, or until tender.

2. Add the rosemary and cook for 2 minutes. Add the white wine and stock and bring to a boil.

3. Reduce heat so that the soup simmers and cook for 30 minutes, or until the vegetables are very tender.

4. Transfer the soup to a food processor, puree until creamy, and then strain through a fine sieve.

5. Place the soup in a clean pan and bring to a simmer. Add the heavy cream and season with salt and pepper.

6. Serve in warm bowls with the Turkey Dumplings.

TURKEY DUMPLINGS

1. Place the bread and parsley in a food processor and pulse until combined. Add the flour and baking powder and blend until combined.

2. Slowly add the milk, egg, and butter to the food processor. Pulse until a paste forms.

3. Fold in the turkey and season with salt and pepper. Refrigerate for 1 hour.

4. Place the Turkey Stock in a medium saucepan. If there is not enough from the recipe above, top off with chicken stock.

5. Drop tablespoon-sized balls of the turkey dumpling mixture into the stock. Cover and cook for 12 minutes. Remove and set aside.

DUTCH PEA SOUP

YIELD: **6 SERVINGS**

ACTIVE TIME: **30 MINUTES**

TOTAL TIME: **: 3 TO 4 HOURS**

INGREDIENTS

2 TABLESPOONS BACON FAT OR UNSALTED BUTTER

½ LB. SALT PORK, MINCED

1 LARGE CARROT, PEELED AND MINCED

1 CELERY STALK, MINCED

½ LARGE YELLOW ONION, MINCED

1 LEEK, WHITE PART ONLY, WASHED AND SLICED THIN

1 BULB OF CELERIAC, PEELED AND DICED (ABOUT 1 ½ CUPS)

2 SMALL POTATOES, PEELED AND DICED

3 TABLESPOONS FRESH THYME LEAVES, CHOPPED, PLUS MORE FOR GARNISH

SALT AND PEPPER, TO TASTE

8 CUPS LOW-SODIUM CHICKEN STOCK

1½ CUPS DRIED GREEN SPLIT PEAS, RINSED

1 LB. KIELBASA, SLICED INTO 1-INCH THICK COINS

DIRECTIONS

1. Place a Dutch oven over medium-high heat and add the bacon fat or butter. Add the salt pork, carrot, celery, onion, leek, celeriac, potatoes, thyme, salt, and pepper and cook for 10 minutes, or until the vegetables start to caramelize.

2. Add the chicken stock and the green split peas and reduce the heat to medium-low. Cook for 2 to 2½ hours, or until the peas have broken down and your spoon can stand up in the pot. Make sure to stir the soup every 15 to 20 minutes to keep it from burning.

3. Top with the kielbasa, garnish with the additional thyme, and serve.

FIVE-SPICE AND CHICKEN RAMEN

YIELD: **4 SERVINGS**

ACTIVE TIME: **15 MINUTES**

TOTAL TIME: **45 MINUTES**

DIRECTIONS

1. In a medium saucepan, add the chicken stock, garlic, ginger, soy sauce, Worcestershire sauce, five-spice powder, and chili powder, and bring to a boil.

2. Reduce heat so that the soup simmers and cook for 5 minutes. Turn off the heat and let stand.

3. Season with sugar, salt, and pepper.

4. Add the sesame oil to a medium sauté pan and cook over medium heat.

5. Bring 4 cups of water to boil in a medium saucepan. Add udon noodles and cook according to manufacturer's instructions.

6. Add the chicken to the sauté pan and cook for 8 minutes, or until browned on all sides.

7. Add the corn kernels to the chicken and cook for 2 minutes. Add the cooked udon noodles and spinach and cook for 1 minute.

8. Strain the broth through a fine sieve, and discard the solids. Place the broth in a clean pan and bring to a boil.

9. Place the udon noodles with the chicken and corn in warm bowls. Pour the broth over the top and garnish with the hardboiled eggs, scallions, and nori.

HARDBOILED EGGS

1. Bring enough water to a boil in medium saucepan so that it will cover eggs by at least 1 inch.

2. Once boiling, reduce to a simmer, add the eggs, and cook for 10 minutes.

3. Remove and refresh in iced water and leave for 10 minutes.

4. Once cooled down, peel and use.

INGREDIENTS

6 CUPS CHICKEN STOCK

4 GARLIC CLOVES, MINCED

2-INCH PIECE OF GINGER, MINCED

½ CUP SOY SAUCE

2 TEASPOONS WORCESTERSHIRE SAUCE

1 TEASPOON FIVE-SPICE POWDER

⅛ TEASPOON CHILI POWDER

1 TABLESPOON SUGAR, OPTIONAL

SALT AND PEPPER, TO TASTE

2 TABLESPOONS SESAME OIL

8 OZ. UDON NOODLES

2 CHICKEN BREASTS, CUT INTO 1-INCH CUBES

1 CUP CORN KERNELS

1 CUP SPINACH

4 HARDBOILED EGGS, HALVED, FOR GARNISH

8 SCALLION GREENS, FOR GARNISH

1 SHEET NORI, SHREDDED, FOR GARNISH

GREEN ASPARAGUS SOUP WITH CURED LEMON SLICES

YIELD: **4 SERVINGS**

ACTIVE TIME: **30 MINUTES**

TOTAL TIME: **1 HOUR**

INGREDIENTS

2 TABLESPOONS UNSALTED BUTTER

1 ONION, CHOPPED

2 CUPS LEEKS, WHITE PART ONLY, CHOPPED

2 CELERY STALKS, CHOPPED

1 LARGE POTATO, PEELED AND CHOPPED

1 BAY LEAF

4 CUPS CHICKEN STOCK

2 TABLESPOONS EXTRA-VIRGIN OLIVE OIL

3 CUPS GREEN ASPARAGUS, QUARTERED, WHITE BOTTOMS DISCARDED

¾ CUP CREAM

SALT AND PEPPER, TO TASTE

TO SERVE:

CURED LEMON SLICES

CURED LEMON SLICES

1 LEMON, THINLY SLICED, SEEDS REMOVED

1 TABLESPOON SALT

3 TABLESPOONS SUGAR

DIRECTIONS

1. In a medium saucepan, add the butter and cook over medium heat until melted. Add the onion, leeks, and celery and cook for 5 minutes, or until soft.

2. Add the potato and bay leaf and cook for 5 minutes. Add the stock, bring to a boil, reduce heat so that the soup simmers, and cook for 15 minutes, or until the potatoes are soft.

3. In a large sauté pan, add the oil and warm over medium-high heat. Add the asparagus and cook for 4 minutes, until nicely green and firm. Reserve 12 of the asparagus tips for garnish.

4. Add the asparagus to the soup and simmer for 5 minutes, or until soft.

5. Transfer the soup to a food processor, puree until smooth, and pass through a fine sieve.

6. Return soup to pan, add cream, and season with salt and pepper. Ladle into warm bowls and garnish with the asparagus tips and Cured Lemon Slices.

CURED LEMON SLICES

1. Spread lemon slices on a baking tray.

2. Combine the salt and sugar in a bowl. Sprinkle half on the lemon slices.

3. Let lemon slices stand for 15 minutes. Flip them over, sprinkle remaining mixture on them, and let stand for 15 minutes.

4. Bring a pot of water to boil. Add the lemon slices and boil for 30 seconds. Submerge in ice water, dry, and set aside until ready to serve.

IRANIAN BARLEY SOUP

YIELD: **4 SERVINGS**

ACTIVE TIME: **20 MINUTES**

TOTAL TIME: **1 HOUR AND 30 MINUTES**

INGREDIENTS

2 TABLESPOONS VEGETABLE OIL

2 ONIONS, CHOPPED

2 CARROTS, PEELED AND CHOPPED

1 CUP PEARL BARLEY

3 TABLESPOONS TOMATO PASTE

1 TEASPOON TURMERIC

8 CUPS CHICKEN STOCK

½ CUP SOUR CREAM

⅓ CUP CHOPPED PARSLEY LEAVES

SALT AND PEPPER, TO TASTE

8 LIME WEDGES

DIRECTIONS

1. In a large saucepan, add the oil and cook over medium heat until warm. Add the onions and cook for 5 minutes, or until soft. Add the carrots, barley, tomato paste, and turmeric and cook for 2 minutes.

2. Add the chicken stock and bring to a boil. Reduce heat so that the soup simmers and cook for 1 hour, or until the barley is tender.

3. Remove from heat. Add the sour cream and parsley, season with salt and pepper, and serve in warm bowls with the lime wedges.

INGREDIENTS

1 THAI CHILI, SEEDS REMOVED AND CHOPPED

2 SHALLOTS, PEELED AND CUT INTO QUARTERS, PLUS MORE FOR GARNISH

4 GARLIC CLOVES, MINCED

1 LEMONGRASS STALK, BRUISED WITH THE BACK OF A KNIFE

1 TEASPOON LIME ZEST

1-INCH PIECE OF GALANGAL ROOT, PEELED AND FINELY CHOPPED

1-INCH PIECE OF GINGER, PEELED AND FINELY CHOPPED

SMALL BUNCH OF CILANTRO, LEAVES REMOVED, STEMS RESERVED

1 TEASPOON CORIANDER SEEDS

1 CARDAMOM POD, SEEDS REMOVED, SHELL DISCARDED

PINCH OF SALT, PLUS MORE TO TASTE

1½ TABLESPOONS SHRIMP PASTE

1 CUP VEGETABLE OIL

4 OZ. RICE NOODLES

2 (14 OZ.) CANS COCONUT MILK

1 CUP CHICKEN STOCK

2 TABLESPOONS SUGAR

4 CHICKEN LEGS, SPLIT INTO DRUMSTICKS AND THIGHS

FISH SAUCE, TO TASTE

PEPPER, TO TASTE

LIME WEDGES, FOR GARNISH

KHAO SOI GAI WITH RICE NOODLES

YIELD: **4 SERVINGS**

ACTIVE TIME: **30 MINUTES**

TOTAL TIME: **1 HOUR**

DIRECTIONS

1. In a nonstick sauté pan, add chili, shallots, garlic, lemongrass, lime zest, galangal root, ginger, cilantro stalks, coriander seeds, and cardamom seeds and cook over low heat for 5 minutes, or until the mixture becomes fragrant.

2. Transfer the contents of the saucepan to a mortar and pestle. Add a pinch of salt and the shrimp paste and grind until a very fine paste is formed. Set aside.

3. Place the vegetable oil in a Dutch oven and cook over medium-high heat until it reaches 325°F.

4. Place 1 ounce of rice noodles into the oil and cook until nice and crispy. Remove with a slotted spoon, set to drain on a paper towel, and season with salt. Reserve for garnish.

5. In a medium saucepan, add 1 tablespoon of the hot vegetable oil and 2 tablespoons of the creamy fat from the top of the coconut milk. Cook over high heat until the coconut fat breaks up and begins to smoke. Add the paste and cook for 45 seconds, while stirring constantly.

6. Reduce heat and whisk in the remaining coconut milk, chicken stock, and sugar.

7. Add the chicken pieces and simmer, while turning the chicken occasionally, for 30 minutes, or until the chicken is tender.

8. In the meantime, bring a pot of salted water to a boil and add the remaining rice noodles. Turn off heat, cover, and let stand for 3 minutes.

9. Place the noodles into warm bowls. Season the soup with fish sauce, salt, and pepper, and pour the soup over the noodles. Garnish with sliced shallots, lime wedges, and crispy rice noodles.

LAMB & BARLEY SOUP

YIELD: **4 TO 6 SERVINGS**

ACTIVE TIME: **20 MINUTES**

TOTAL TIME: **1 HOUR AND 15 MINUTES**

INGREDIENTS

2 TABLESPOONS EXTRA-VIRGIN
OLIVE OIL

1 ONION, PEELED AND CHOPPED

2 CARROTS, PEELED AND CHOPPED

2 CELERY STALKS, CHOPPED

1½ LBS. GROUND LAMB

2 THYME SPRIGS, LEAVES REMOVED
AND CHOPPED

2 (14 OZ.) CANS TOMATOES

3 CUPS LAMB STOCK

3 CUPS VEAL OR BEEF STOCK

½ CUP PEARL BARLEY

½ TEASPOON CUMIN

½ TEASPOON CHILI POWDER

¼ CUP CHOPPED PARSLEY LEAVES

SALT AND PEPPER, TO TASTE

DIRECTIONS

1. In a medium saucepan, add the olive oil and cook over medium heat until warm.

2. Add the onion, carrots, and celery and cook for 5 minutes, or until soft.

3. Add the ground lamb and cook for 5 minutes, or until evenly browned.

4. Add the thyme, tomatoes, stock, barley, cumin, and chili powder and bring to a boil. Reduce heat so that the soup simmers and cook for 30 minutes, or until barley is tender.

5. Fold in the parsley. Season with salt and pepper and serve in warmed bowls.

LAMB AND CANNELLINI SOUP

YIELD: **4 TO 6 SERVINGS**

ACTIVE TIME: **20 MINUTES**

TOTAL TIME: **13 HOURS AND 30 MINUTES**

INGREDIENTS

2 TABLESPOONS EXTRA-VIRGIN
OLIVE OIL

1 ONION, CHOPPED

2 GARLIC CLOVES, MINCED

1½ LBS. GROUND LAMB

3 CARROTS, PEELED AND CHOPPED

3 CELERY STALKS, CHOPPED

1 (14 OZ.) CAN STEWED TOMATOES

¼ CUP PARSLEY, LEAVES REMOVED
AND CHOPPED

2 SPRIGS THYME, LEAVES REMOVED
AND CHOPPED

8 OZ. CANNELLINI BEANS, SOAKED
IN WATER OVERNIGHT

6 CUPS CHICKEN STOCK

8 OZ. BABY SPINACH

¼ CUP SLICED KALAMATA OLIVES

SALT AND PEPPER, TO TASTE

FETA CHEESE, FOR GARNISH

DIRECTIONS

1. In a large saucepan, add the oil and cook over medium heat until warm.

2. Add the onion and cook for 5 minutes, or until soft.

3. Add the garlic and cook for an additional 2 minutes.

4. Add the lamb and cook for 3 to 4 minutes. Add the carrots and celery, and cook for an additional 5 minutes.

5. Stir in the tomatoes, herbs, cannellini beans, and chicken stock. Bring to a boil, reduce heat so that the soup simmers, cover, and cook for 1 hour, or until the beans are tender.

6. Add the spinach and olives. Cook for 2 minutes, or until spinach is wilted.

7. Season with salt and pepper and serve in warmed bowls with a sprinkle of feta cheese.

LEEK & FISH SOUP

YIELD: **4 TO 6 SERVINGS**

ACTIVE TIME: **30 MINUTES**

TOTAL TIME: **1 HOUR**

DIRECTIONS

1. Add the oil to a medium saucepan and cook over medium heat until warm. Add the leeks, crushed coriander seeds, and chili flakes and cook for 5 minutes.

2. Add potatoes and tomatoes. Pour in the stock and the wine, add the bay leaves, star anise, orange zest, and saffron and bring to a boil. Reduce heat so that the soup simmers and cook for 15 minutes, or until the potatoes are tender.

3. Taste and adjust the seasoning. Add the fish and the squid to the soup and cook for 3 to 4 minutes. Add the shrimp and cook for 2 minutes.

4. Serve in warm bowls with Parsley Grilled Baguette, Garlic Mayonnaise, and microgreens.

GARLIC MAYONNAISE

1. Combine the egg yolk, garlic, vinegar, water, and mustard in a stainless steel bowl. Whisk until foamy.

2. Gradually add the oils in a thin stream, constantly whisking until all of the oils have been incorporated and the mayonnaise is thick.

3. Season with lemon juice, salt, and pepper. Refrigerate immediately.

PARSLEY GRILLED BAGUETTE

1. In a large sauté pan, add 2 tablespoons of the butter and cook over medium heat until melted.

2. Add 4 slices of the baguette and cook for 1 minute, flip, sprinkle half of the chopped parsley on, and cook for another minute.

3. Flip the pieces of bread and cook the side with the parsley on it for 30 seconds.

4. Repeat with the remaining 4 slices of baguette.

INGREDIENTS

2 TABLESPOONS EXTRA-VIRGIN OLIVE OIL

2 LEEKS, WHITE PART ONLY, CUT INTO ⅛-INCH SLICES

2 TEASPOONS CORIANDER SEEDS, CRUSHED

⅛ TEASPOON CHILI FLAKES

3 CUPS MULTICOLORED LITTLE CREAMER POTATOES, CUT INTO ¼-INCH SLICES

1 (14 OZ.) CAN DICED TOMATOES

4 CUPS FISH STOCK

1 CUP WHITE WINE

2 BAY LEAVES

1 STAR ANISE

ZEST OF 1 ORANGE

⅛ TEASPOON SAFFRON

1 LB. COD FILLET, CUT INTO ½-INCH PIECES

1 LB. SMALL SQUID, BODIES HALVED AND SCORED, TENTACLES LEFT WHOLE

10 OZ. SHRIMP, PEELED AND DEVEINED

SALT AND PEPPER, TO TASTE

TO SERVE:

GARLIC MAYONNAISE

PARSLEY GRILLED BAGUETTE

MICROGREENS

GARLIC MAYONNAISE

1 EGG YOLK

4 GARLIC CLOVES, MASHED TO A PASTE

1 TABLESPOON WHITE VINEGAR

1 TABLESPOON WATER

½ TEASPOON DRY MUSTARD

1 CUP VEGETABLE OIL

½ CUP EXTRA-VIRGIN OLIVE OIL

1 TEASPOON LEMON JUICE

SALT AND PEPPER, TO TASTE

PARSLEY GRILLED BAGUETTE

4 TABLESPOONS UNSALTED BUTTER

8 SLICES BAGUETTE

1 TABLESPOON CHOPPED PARSLEY LEAVES

LEFTOVER TURKEY PASTA SOUP

YIELD: **4 SERVINGS**

ACTIVE TIME: **20 MINUTES**

TOTAL TIME: **45 MINUTES**

INGREDIENTS

1 TABLESPOON EXTRA-VIRGIN OLIVE OIL

1 ONION, CHOPPED

2 CELERY STALKS, CHOPPED

2 CARROTS, PEELED AND CHOPPED

6 CUPS TURKEY STOCK

1 BAY LEAF

1 TEASPOON CHOPPED ROSEMARY LEAVES

½ CUP ORZO

2 CUPS COOKED AND CHOPPED TURKEY

1 TEASPOON CHOPPED PARSLEY LEAVES

SALT AND PEPPER, TO TASTE

DIRECTIONS

1. In a medium saucepan, warm oil over medium heat. Add the onion, celery, and carrots and cook for 5 minutes, or until soft.

2. Add the stock, bay leaf, and rosemary and bring to a boil.

3. Reduce heat so that the soup simmers and cook for 10 minutes.

4. Add the orzo and simmer for 8 to 10 minutes, or until the pasta is tender.

5. Add the turkey meat and parsley. Season with salt and pepper, and serve in warm bowls.

LEMON TURKEY COUSCOUS SOUP

YIELD: **4 SERVINGS**

ACTIVE TIME: **20 MINUTES**

TOTAL TIME: **1 HOUR**

INGREDIENTS

2 TABLESPOONS EXTRA-VIRGIN OLIVE OIL

1 ONION, CHOPPED

2 GARLIC CLOVES

2 CARROTS, PEELED AND FINELY CHOPPED

2 CELERY STALKS, FINELY CHOPPED

⅓ CUP CHOPPED RED BELL PEPPER

⅓ CUP CHOPPED GREEN BELL PEPPER

6 CUPS TURKEY STOCK

ZEST AND JUICE OF 1 LEMON

½ CUP ISRAELI COUSCOUS

2 CUPS COOKED TURKEY MEAT, CHOPPED

4 CUPS SPINACH

SALT AND PEPPER, TO TASTE

DIRECTIONS

1. In a medium saucepan, add the olive oil and cook over medium heat until warm. Add the onion and cook for 5 minutes, or until soft.

2. Add the garlic and cook for 2 minutes. Add the carrots, celery, and bell peppers and cook for 5 minutes, or until tender. Add the stock, lemon zest, and couscous and bring to a boil.

3. Reduce heat so that the soup simmers and cook for 15 minutes.

4. Add the cooked turkey and lemon juice and simmer for 5 minutes.

5. Add the spinach and cook for 2 minutes, or until it wilts. Season with salt and pepper and serve in warm bowls.

YIELD: **4 SERVINGS**

ACTIVE TIME: **30 MINUTES**

TOTAL TIME: **2 HOURS AND 30 MINUTES**

INGREDIENTS

2 CHICKEN THIGHS

8 CUPS CHICKEN STOCK

1-INCH PIECE OF GINGER, SLICED

3 LEMONGRASS STALKS, CUT IN HALF AND BRUISED WITH THE BACK SIDE OF A KNIFE

1 THAI CHILI WITH SEEDS

3 TABLESPOONS FISH SAUCE

½ CUP LONG-GRAIN RICE, RINSED

CHILI, CUT INTO THIN STRIPS, FOR GARNISH

CHOPPED CILANTRO, FOR GARNISH

LIME WEDGES, FOR GARNISH

TO SERVE:

NAAN

NAAN

½ TEASPOON YEAST

1 CUP WARM WATER

2 TABLESPOONS SUGAR

1 TABLESPOON MILK

1 EGG

1 TEASPOON SALT

2 CUPS BREAD FLOUR

½ CUP UNSALTED BUTTER, MELTED

LEMONGRASS-SCENTED CHICKEN AND RICE SOUP

DIRECTIONS

1. In a large saucepan add the chicken thighs, chicken stock, ginger, lemongrass, Thai chiles, and fish sauce.

2. Bring to a boil and simmer for 2 hours or until the chicken legs are tender.

3. Skim off any fat.

4. Remove the chicken legs and pick apart the meat. Discard the skin and bones.

5. Strain the stock through a fine sieve.

6. Reboil stock, stir in the rice, and simmer for 30 minutes, or until rice is cooked.

7. Remove chili, add chicken leg meat until hot, and serve.

8. Garnish with thinly sliced chili, chopped cilantro, and lime wedges and serve with Naan.

NAAN

1. Combine the yeast and warm water in a bowl and let stand for 10 minutes.

2. In a separate bowl, combine the yeast mixture, sugar, milk, egg, salt, and bread flour and mix by hand until it is formed into a ball of dough.

3. On a lightly floured surface, knead the dough for 5 minutes. Place the dough in a bowl, cover it with a towel, and let stand for 30 to 45 minutes in a warm place, until it doubles in size.

4. Cut into 4 pieces and roll on a lightly floured surface. Each piece should be ¼ inch thick.

5. Brush both sides with melted butter and cook on a grill until golden brown. Remove from grill and brush the tops with melted butter before serving.

MACARONI AND CHEESE SOUP

YIELD: **4 SERVINGS**

ACTIVE TIME: **15 MINUTES**

TOTAL TIME: **40 MINUTES**

INGREDIENTS

1½ CUPS ELBOW PASTA

¼ CUP UNSALTED BUTTER

1 ONION, PEELED AND CHOPPED

2 CARROTS, PEELED AND CHOPPED

2 CELERY STALKS, CHOPPED

2 TABLESPOONS ALL-PURPOSE
FLOUR

4 CUPS CHICKEN STOCK

2 CUPS MILK

4 CUPS GRATED SHARP CHEDDAR
CHEESE

SALT AND PEPPER, TO TASTE

DIRECTIONS

1. Cook the pasta according to the manufacturer's instructions. Drain and set aside.

2. In a medium saucepan, add the butter and cook over low heat until it is melted.

3. Add the onion, carrots, and celery. Stirring frequently, cook for 5 minutes, or until the vegetables are soft.

4. Add the flour and cook for 5 minutes.

5. Add the chicken stock and milk and bring to a boil. Reduce heat so that the soup simmers and cook for 10 minutes.

6. Remove pan from heat and add the grated cheddar cheese. Mix together with a whisk.

7. Season with salt and pepper, add cooked pasta, and serve in bowls.

INGREDIENTS

2 TABLESPOONS SESAME OIL

4 GARLIC CLOVES, MINCED

2-INCH PIECE OF GINGER, PEELED AND MINCED

2 SHALLOTS, FINELY CHOPPED

8 OZ. GROUND PORK

2 TEASPOON CHILI BEAN PASTE

6 TABLESPOONS MISO

4 TABLESPOONS SESAME SEEDS, MIXTURE OF BLACK AND WHITE, TOASTED AND GROUND INTO A PASTE

2 TABLESPOONS SUGAR

2 TABLESPOONS SAKE

8 CUPS CHICKEN STOCK

SALT AND PEPPER, TO TASTE

NOODLES FROM 2 PACKETS OF RAMEN

PICKLED RED GINGER, FOR GARNISH

POACHED EGGS, FOR GARNISH

TO SERVE:

SPICY BEAN SPROUT SALAD

SPICY BEAN SPROUT SALAD

12 OZ. BEAN SPROUTS

1 TABLESPOON BLACK SESAME SEEDS

2 GREEN ONIONS, THINLY SLICED

2 TABLESPOONS SESAME OIL

2 TEASPOONS SOY SAUCE

⅛ TEASPOON RED CHILI FLAKES

PINCH OF GROUND GINGER

ZEST OF 1 ORANGE

MISO RAMEN WITH SPICY BEAN SPROUT SALAD

YIELD: **4 SERVINGS**

ACTIVE TIME: **20 MINUTES**

TOTAL TIME: **45 MINUTES**

DIRECTIONS

1. In a medium saucepan, warm the sesame oil over medium heat. Add the garlic, ginger, and shallots and cook for 3 minutes, or until fragrant.

2. Increase the heat to medium-high and add the ground pork. Cook for 5 minutes, or until nicely browned. Add the chili bean paste, miso, sesame paste, sugar, sake, and chicken stock and stir to combine.

3. Bring to a boil. Reduce heat so that the soup simmers and season with salt and pepper.

4. Cook the noodles according to manufacturer's instructions.

5. Place the noodles in warm bowls. Pour the soup over the noodles and garnish with the Spicy Bean Sprout Salad, pickled red ginger, and poached eggs.

SPICY BEAN SPROUT SALAD

1. Bring a pot of water to a boil. Add the bean sprouts and cook for 2 minutes. Remove, strain through a fine sieve, and let cool.

2. Combine the remaining ingredients together in a bowl. Add the cooled bean sprouts, mix gently until combined, and serve.

POACHED EGGS

1. Crack each egg into a small, individual bowl.

2. In a medium saucepan, add 3 cups water and 2 tablespoons white vinegar and bring to a boil.

3. Reduce the heat so that the water simmers and gently add the eggs to the water one at a time.

4. Cook for 3 minutes, gently basting the eggs with the poaching water as they cook.

5. Gently remove the eggs with a slotted spoon and place on a paper towel to dry.

6. Season each egg with salt and pepper and serve immediately.

MOROCCAN LEGUME SOUP WITH HONEY BUNS

YIELD: **4 SERVINGS**

ACTIVE TIME: **45 MINUTES**

TOTAL TIME: **13 HOURS**

DIRECTIONS

1. In a medium saucepan, add the oil and cook over medium heat until warm. Add the onions and cook for 5 minutes, or until soft.

2. Add the ginger, turmeric, cinnamon, saffron threads, tomatoes, and sugar. Stir in the chickpeas and the stock and bring to a boil. Reduce heat so that the soup simmers, cover, and cook for 10 minutes.

3. Add the lentils and fava beans and continue to cook for 15 minutes, or until all the legumes are tender. Add the cilantro and parsley, season with salt and pepper, and serve in warmed bowls with Honey Buns.

HONEY BUNS

1. Combine the yeast and approximately 1 tablespoon of lukewarm water in a bowl and let stand until yeast is dissolved.

2. Sieve the flour and salt into a mixing bowl. Add the dissolved yeast, honey, and fennel seeds, then slowly add 1 cup of milk. Stir until well-combined.

3. Place the dough on a floured work surface and knead for 5 minutes, until it is smooth and elastic.

4. Cover the dough with a damp cloth and let stand until it has doubled in size.

5. Preheat the oven to 450°F.

6. Divide the dough into 12 pieces and shape each piece into a ball.

7. Place on a baking tray and let stand for 10 minutes.

8. Combine the egg yolk and 1 tablespoon of milk in a small bowl. Brush the top of each bun with the egg mixture, sprinkle on the poppy seeds, if using, and place in the oven. Bake for 15 minutes, or until golden brown on top and bottom.

9. Remove the buns from the tray and place on a wire rack to cool.

INGREDIENTS

1½ TABLESPOONS EXTRA-VIRGIN
    OLIVE OIL

1 ONION, PEELED, HALVED, AND
    SLICED

¼ TEASPOON GROUND GINGER

¼ TEASPOON TURMERIC

½ TEASPOON CINNAMON

⅛ TEASPOON SAFFRON THREADS

1 (14 OZ.) CAN DICED TOMATOES

1 TEASPOON SUGAR

½ CUP CHICKPEAS, SOAKED
    OVERNIGHT AND STRAINED

4 CUPS VEAL STOCK

⅓ CUP BROWN LENTILS, SOAKED
    OVERNIGHT AND STRAINED

½ CUP DRIED FAVA BEANS, SOAKED
    OVERNIGHT AND STRAINED

1 TABLESPOON CHOPPED CILANTRO
    LEAVES

1 TABLESPOON CHOPPED PARSLEY
    LEAVES

SALT AND PEPPER, TO TASTE

TO SERVE:

HONEY BUNS

HONEY BUNS

½ TEASPOON DRIED YEAST

1¾ CUPS BREAD FLOUR

½ TEASPOON SALT

2 TABLESPOONS HONEY

1 TEASPOON FENNEL SEEDS

1 CUP MILK, PLUS 1 TABLESPOON

1 EGG YOLK

1 TEASPOON POPPY SEEDS
    (OPTIONAL)

PARSNIP & PEAR SOUP

YIELD: **4 TO 6 SERVINGS**

ACTIVE TIME: **30 MINUTES**

TOTAL TIME: **1 HOUR AND 15 MINUTES**

INGREDIENTS

2 TABLESPOONS UNSALTED BUTTER

4 CUPS PEELED AND DICED
  PARSNIPS

1 ONION, CHOPPED

1 CUP PEELED AND DICED PEAR

1 GARLIC CLOVE, MINCED

1 THYME SPRIG, CHOPPED

½ CUP WHITE WINE

8 CUPS CHICKEN STOCK

BLUE CHEESE CRUMBLES, FOR
  GARNISH

TO SERVE:

POACHED PEARS

POACHED PEARS

1 CUP RED WINE

¼ CUP SUGAR

1 TEASPOON LEMON JUICE

1 CINNAMON STICK

1 STAR ANISE

1 PEAR, PEELED AND FINELY
  CHOPPED

DIRECTIONS

1. In a medium saucepan, add the butter and cook over medium heat until melted. Add the parsnip, onion, pear, garlic, and thyme and cook for 10 minutes, or until soft, stirring often.

2. Add the wine and cook until it has evaporated.

3. Add the chicken stock. Simmer for 30 minutes, or until the parsnip is tender.

4. Transfer the soup to a food processor, puree until smooth, and strain through a fine sieve.

5. Adjust the seasoning. Ladle into warm bowls, serve with the Poached Pears, and garnish with blue cheese.

POACHED PEARS

1. In a small saucepan, add the wine, sugar, lemon juice, cinnamon stick, and star anise. Bring to a boil, remove from heat, and let stand.

2. Add the chopped pear and return to a boil.

3. Remove from heat and let the pear cool in the mixture. It is best to let sit in the refrigerator overnight. Remove pear with a slotted spoon and serve.

PORK & CRAB WONTON SOUP

YIELD: **4 SERVINGS**

ACTIVE TIME: **40 MINUTES**

TOTAL TIME: **1 HOUR**

DIRECTIONS

1. In a medium saucepan, add the sesame oil and cook over medium heat until warm. Add the onion and carrots and cook for 5 minutes, or until soft.

2. Add the garlic and cook for 2 minutes. Add mirin, crab stock, lemongrass, soy sauce, and fish sauce. Simmer for 10 minutes, and then remove the lemongrass.

3. Bring the soup to a boil and add the Pork and Crab Wontons. Reduce heat so that the soup simmers and cook for 5 minutes, or until the wontons float to the top.

4. Place 3 wontons in each bowl, pour the soup over the wantons, and garnish with toasted sesame seeds, cilantro, sesame oil, and the broken nori.

PORK AND CRAB WONTONS

1. Combine all ingredients in a bowl, except the wonton wrappers, and mix until well combined.

2. Place 2 teaspoons of the mixture in the center of a wonton wrapper.

3. Dip a finger into cold water and rub it around the entire edge of the wonton. Bring each corner of the wrapper together and seal together. Repeat with remaining wonton wrappers and refrigerate until ready to use.

INGREDIENTS

1 TABLESPOON SESAME OIL , PLUS MORE FOR GARNISH

1 ONION, FINELY CHOPPED

2 CARROTS, FINELY CHOPPED

2 GARLIC CLOVES, FINELY CHOPPED

1 CUP MIRIN

4 CUPS CRAB STOCK

1 LEMONGRASS STALK, BRUISED WITH THE BACK OF A KNIFE

1 TABLESPOON SOY SAUCE

1 TABLESPOON FISH SAUCE

12 WONTONS

SESAME SEEDS, TOASTED, FOR GARNISH

CILANTRO, CHOPPED, FOR GARNISH

1 SHEET OF NORI, BROKEN, FOR GARNISH

PORK AND CRAB WONTONS

4 OZ. CRAB MEAT, CLEANED, COOKED, FINELY CHOPPED

4 OZ. GROUND PORK

1 TABLESPOON MINCED SHALLOTS

1 TABLESPOON CHOPPED CHIVES

1 TABLESPOON FISH SAUCE

2 TABLESPOONS MISO

2 TABLESPOONS CHOPPED RADISH

1 TABLESPOON SESAME SEEDS, TOASTED

1 TEASPOON SESAME OIL

1 TEASPOON SHERRY

12 WONTON WRAPPERS

PORK BELLY & SWEET CORN CHOWDER

YIELD: **6 SERVINGS**

ACTIVE TIME: **25 MINUTES**

TOTAL TIME: **30 HOURS**

INGREDIENTS

1 LB. PORK BELLY

1 TABLESPOON SEA SALT

6 TABLESPOONS UNSALTED BUTTER

1 LARGE ONION, DICED

1 CUP DICED, COOKED BACON

2 CELERY STALKS, CHOPPED

2 GARLIC CLOVES, MINCED

¼ CUP ALL-PURPOSE FLOUR

3 CUPS FRESH CORN KERNELS

2 LARGE POTATOES, CHOPPED

3 SPRIGS FRESH THYME

½ CUP CREAM

½ CUP WHOLE MILK

SMOKED PAPRIKA, FOR GARNISH

DIRECTIONS

1. The day before you plan on serving this recipe, rub the pork belly with salt, put the meat on a metal rack over a dish, and refrigerate overnight.

2. The next day, pour boiling water over the pork belly. Leave it to cool and drain.

3. Preheat the oven to 300°F.

4. Pat the skin dry, sprinkle with more salt, and roast for 3 hours. After 3 hours, remove the pork from the oven and raise the temperature to 500°F.

5. Using a knife, remove the skin from the pork to make cracklings. Once skin is removed, cover the pork with foil and let rest.

6. To make cracklings, place the skin on a baking tray and cook it in the oven for 20 to 25 minutes, or until the skin is puffed and crisp. Set aside.

7. In a large saucepan over medium-high heat, melt butter then add onion, sautéing until slightly golden. Add bacon, celery, and garlic, stirring often for 5 minutes.

8. Add the flour to the saucepan and continue to stir, making sure to fully incorporate the flour into the mixture.

9. Add the corn, potatoes, thyme, cream, and milk and simmer until the potatoes are fork tender. Season to taste.

10. To serve, ladle soup into bowls, top with sliced pork belly, and garnish with paprika and the cracklings.

PORK TERIYAKI & RED MISO RAMEN

YIELD: **6 SERVINGS**

ACTIVE TIME: **30 MINUTES**

TOTAL TIME: **2 HOURS AND 30 MINUTES**

INGREDIENTS

1½ LBS. PORK BONES

1 ONION, CHOPPED

2-INCH PIECE OF GINGER, PEELED AND MINCED

¼ CUP SOY SAUCE

1 CUP MIRIN

1 TABLESPOON BROWN SUGAR

1 CUP WATER

3 TABLESPOONS VEGETABLE OIL

1 ¼ LBS. PORK TENDERLOIN, CHOPPED INTO 1-INCH PIECES

⅔ CUP RED MISO

4 SCALLIONS, SLICED

SALT AND PEPPER, TO TASTE

BAMBOO SHOOTS, FOR GARNISH

6 HARDBOILED EGGS, HALVED, FOR GARNISH

NORI, FOR GARNISH

TO SERVE:

BUTTERED CORN KERNELS

COOKED BEAN SPROUTS AND NOODLES

CHILI-GARLIC OIL

BUTTERED CORN KERNELS

2 TABLESPOONS UNSALTED BUTTER

1 CUP CORN KERNELS, COOKED

SALT AND PEPPER, TO TASTE

COOKED BEAN SPROUTS AND NOODLES

8 OZ. BEAN SPROUTS

12 OZ. RAMEN NOODLES

1 TABLESPOON SESAME OIL

CHILI-GARLIC OIL

¼ CUP VEGETABLE OIL

3 GARLIC CLOVES, MINCED

1 TEASPOON RED PEPPER FLAKES

SOY SAUCE, TO TASTE

DIRECTIONS

1. In a stockpot, bring 8 cups of water to boil. Add the pork bones and boil for 5 minutes.

2. Remove the bones, discard the water, and clean the pot.

3. Bring 12 cups of water to boil and add the pork bones, onion, and ginger. Reduce heat so that the water simmers and cook for 1 hour and 30 minutes.

4. In a mixing bowl, add the soy sauce, mirin, brown sugar, and water. Stir until combined and then set aside.

5. In a large sauté pan, add 2 tablespoons of the oil and warm over medium-high heat.

6. Add the pork tenderloin and cook for 5 minutes, or until browned on all sides.

7. Pour the contents of the mixing bowl into the pan, reduce heat to low, and cook for 25 minutes, stirring halfway through.

8. Remove pan from heat and let cool.

9. While waiting for stock to finish cooking, prepare the Chili-Garlic Oil, Buttered Corn Kernels, and Cooked Bean Sprouts and Noodles (see at right).

10. When the stock is done cooking, strain through a fine sieve. Add 1 cup of the stock

to a clean pan and bring to a boil. Remove the pan from heat and add the red miso.

11. In a medium saucepan, add the remaining vegetable oil and warm over medium-high heat.

12. Add the scallions and sauté for 1 minute. Add the remaining stock and bring to a boil.

13. Reduce heat to low and add the miso. Mix until combined and then shut off the heat. Season with salt and pepper.

14. Place the pork, hardboiled eggs, Buttered Corn Kernels, and Cooked Bean Sprouts and Noodles into warm bowls. Pour the broth on top and then garnish with bamboo shoots, nori, and Chili-Garlic Oil.

BUTTERED CORN KERNELS

1. In a small saucepan, add the butter and cook over medium heat until warm. Add the corn, cook for 3 minutes, and season with salt and pepper. Set aside until ready to serve.

COOKED BEAN SPROUTS AND NOODLES

1. Bring 8 cups of water to a boil in a large saucepan. Add

the sprouts, boil for 1 minute, remove, and set aside.

2. Add the noodles and cook according to manufacturer's instructions. Remove noodles from the pan and place in a mixing bowl. Add the bean sprouts and the sesame oil, stir until combined, and set aside.

CHILE-GARLIC OIL

1. In a small saucepan, add the oil and warm over low heat.

2. After 2 minutes, add the garlic and red pepper flakes and cook for an additional 2 minutes.

3. Remove from heat, let cool, and season with soy sauce.

4. Stir to combine and reserve until ready to use.

HARDBOILED EGGS

1. Bring enough water to a boil in medium saucepan so that it will cover eggs by at least 1 inch.

2. Once boiling, reduce to a simmer, add the eggs, and cook for 10 minutes.

3. Remove and refresh in iced water and leave for 10 minutes.

4. Once cooled down, peel and use.

YIELD: **10 SERVINGS**

ACTIVE TIME: **1 HOUR**

TOTAL TIME: **3 HOURS**

POZOLE BLANCO

INGREDIENTS

1½ LBS. DRIED HOMINY, SOAKED OVERNIGHT

16 CUPS WATER, PLUS MORE AS NEEDED

½ OZ. CALCIUM OXIDE

1 TABLESPOON KOSHER SALT, PLUS MORE TO TASTE

2 LB. PORK BUTT, CUT INTO 2-INCH CUBES

2 LBS. BONE-IN, SKIN-ON CHICKEN

1 ONION, HALVED

1 HEAD OF GARLIC

RADISHES, SLICED THIN, FOR SERVING

GREEN CABBAGE, FINELY SHREDDED, FOR SERVING

LIME WEDGES, FOR SERVING

SALSA OR HOT SAUCE, FOR SERVING

DIRECTIONS

1. Drain the hominy and place it in a large saucepan. Add the water, calcium oxide, and salt and bring to a boil. Cook for 30 minutes.

2. Drain the hominy and run it under cold water, rubbing the hominy between your hands to remove the loosened husks. Set the hominy aside.

3. Place the pork and chicken in a large saucepan. Fill the pan with water until it is no less than 2 inches from the top. Add the onion and garlic, season with salt, and bring to a simmer. Reduce the heat to low and cook until the pork and chicken are tender and falling apart, about 2 hours.

4. Remove the chicken from the pot. Remove the bones and skin and save the bones for another preparation.

5. Use a strainer to remove the garlic skins from the broth. Return the chicken to the pot, add the hominy, and cook for another 30 minutes.

6. Ladle the pozole into warmed bowls and serve with radish, cabbage, lime wedges, and salsa.

ROASTED CORN & RED PEPPER BISQUE WITH BACON

YIELD: **3 TO 5 SERVINGS**

ACTIVE TIME: **30 MINUTES**

TOTAL TIME: **40 MINUTES**

INGREDIENTS

½ LB. BACON, DICED

3 CUPS FRESH CORN KERNELS

2 TABLESPOONS OLIVE OIL

SALT AND PEPPER, TO TASTE

3 RED BELL PEPPERS

½ CUP HEAVY CREAM

½ CUP MILK

1½ STICKS UNSALTED BUTTER, DIVIDED

DIRECTIONS

1. Preheat the oven to 375°F.

2. Add bacon to a saucepan over medium heat and cook until brown. Using a slotted spoon, set bacon on a paper towel-lined plate.

3. On a baking sheet, spread out the corn in a thin layer, drizzle oil over it, sprinkle with salt, and bake for 12 minutes, or until the corn starts to darken in color.

4. Remove corn and turn the oven up to 425°F. Roast the peppers until they are charred on all sides. Let the peppers cool in a covered bowl. Once cool, remove the charred skin.

5. In a medium pot, combine the corn, cream, milk, roasted pepper flesh, and butter. Simmer over medium heat for 15 to 20 minutes, stirring to prevent the milk from scalding.

6. Remove the corn mixture from the heat and allow it to cool for 10 minutes.

7. Blend the corn mixture in a blender until smooth.

8. Warm the mixture if it cooled down too much; if not, serve hot. Top with the crumbled bacon.

SAFFRON & MUSSEL BROTH

YIELD: **4 TO 6 SERVINGS**

ACTIVE TIME: **20 MINUTES**

TOTAL TIME: **45 MINUTES**

INGREDIENTS

3 LBS. MUSSELS, RINSED AND SCRUBBED

3 CUPS WHITE WINE

¼ CUP UNSALTED BUTTER

4 CUPS CHOPPED LEEKS

2 CELERY STALKS, CHOPPED

¾ CUP FENNEL, CHOPPED

1 CARROT, FINELY CHOPPED

2 GARLIC CLOVES, MINCED

⅛ TEASPOON SAFFRON

2 CUPS HEAVY CREAM

SALT AND PEPPER, TO TASTE

3 TOMATOES, CONCASSE (SEE PAGE 339) AND CHOPPED

¼ CUP PARSLEY, LEAVES REMOVED AND CHOPPED, FOR GARNISH

MICROGREENS, FOR GARNISH

RADISH, SHAVED, DRESSED WITH OLIVE OIL AND A SQUEEZE OF LEMON JUICE, FOR GARNISH

DIRECTIONS

1. Place the mussels and the wine in a large saucepan, cover, and cook, while shaking the pan occasionally, over medium heat for 4 to 5 minutes, or until all the mussels are open. Discard any unopened mussels.

2. Strain, set the mussels aside, and reserve the cooking liquid.

3. Remove the meat from the mussels. Keep 18 mussels in the shell and reserve for garnish.

4. Add the butter to a large saucepan and cook over medium heat until melted. Add the leeks, celery, fennel, carrot, and garlic and cook for 5 minutes, or until soft.

5. Strain the reserved liquid through a fine sieve, cheesecloth, or coffee filter.

6. Add the reserved liquid to the saucepan with the vegetables. Reduce the heat and cook for 10 minutes to reduce the liquid.

7. Add the saffron and the cream and bring to a boil.

8. Season with salt and pepper. Add the mussels, tomatoes, and parsley and cook gently until heated through.

9. Ladle into bowls and garnish with microgreens, radish, and the reserved mussels.

SAFFRON & SUNCHOKE SOUP

YIELD: **4 SERVINGS**

ACTIVE TIME: **30 MINUTES**

TOTAL TIME: **1 HOUR AND 30 MINUTES**

INGREDIENTS

2 TABLESPOONS EXTRA-VIRGIN
OLIVE OIL

1 ONION, DICED

1 GARLIC CLOVE, MINCED

2 CUPS PEELED AND CHOPPED
SUNCHOKES

4 CUPS CHICKEN STOCK

PINCH OF SAFFRON, PLUS MORE
FOR GARNISH

JUICE OF ½ LEMON

PARSLEY, CHOPPED, FOR GARNISH

TOASTED ALMONDS, FOR GARNISH

TO SERVE:

SUNCHOKE AIOLI AND CRISPY
SKINS

**SUNCHOKE AIOLI AND CRISPY
SKINS**

2 SUNCHOKES

2 EGG YOLKS

½ GARLIC CLOVE, MINCED

½ TEASPOON DIJON MUSTARD

1 TEASPOON LEMON JUICE

½ CUP EXTRA-VIRGIN OLIVE OIL

SALT AND PEPPER, TO TASTE

DIRECTIONS

1. In a medium saucepan, add the oil and cook over medium heat until warm. Add the onion and cook for 5 minutes, or until soft.

2. Add the garlic and sunchokes and cook for 5 minutes. Add the chicken stock and bring to a boil. Reduce heat so that the soup simmers and cook for 15 minutes.

3. Add the saffron and lemon juice. Cook for 15 minutes, or until the sunchokes are soft.

4. Transfer the soup to a food processor, puree, and then pass through a fine sieve.

5. Return the soup to the pan and bring to a simmer.

6. Serve in warm bowls sprinkled with chopped parsley, toasted whole almonds, and saffron threads and serve with Sunchoke Aioli and Crispy Skins.

SUNCHOKE AIOLI AND CRISPY SKINS

1. Preheat the oven to 200°F.

2. In a small saucepan, add the sunchokes and cover with water.

3. Boil for 20 to 25 minutes, or until interior flesh is very tender.

4. Remove from boiling water and submerge in ice water. Remove, cut sunchokes in half, and remove meat with a spoon. Set aside.

5. Place the skins in the oven and cook for 20 minutes, or until crispy. Remove and let cool.

6. Meanwhile, mash the sunchoke meat with a fork. Add the egg yolks, garlic, mustard, and lemon juice, and whisk vigorously until the mixture is nice and smooth.

7. Slowly drizzle in the oil, while whisking constantly. Season with salt and pepper, and serve with Crispy Skins.

INGREDIENTS

1 TABLESPOON SESAME OIL

1 ONION, FINELY CHOPPED

2 CARROTS, FINELY CHOPPED

2 GARLIC CLOVES, FINELY CHOPPED

1 CUP SAKE

4 CUPS FISH STOCK

1 STALK LEMONGRASS, SMASHED WITH THE BACK OF A KNIFE

1 TABLESPOON SOY SAUCE

SALT AND PEPPER, TO TASTE

1 TABLESPOON FISH SAUCE

12 SEAFOOD WONTONS (SEE RECIPE)

1 ROMAINE LETTUCE LEAF, SHREDDED, FOR GARNISH

TOASTED SESAME SEEDS, FOR GARNISH

CILANTRO, CHOPPED, FOR GARNISH

RADISH, SHAVED, FOR GARNISH

SEAFOOD WONTONS

4 OZ. RAW SHRIMP, PEELED, DEVEINED, AND FINELY CHOPPED

4 OZ. COOKED CRAB, CLEANED AND FINELY CHOPPED

1 TABLESPOON CHOPPED SCALLIONS

1 TABLESPOON CHOPPED CHIVES

1 TABLESPOON FISH SAUCE

2 TABLESPOONS MISO

1 TABLESPOON SHRIMP PASTE

2 TABLESPOONS CHOPPED RADISH

1 TABLESPOON SESAME SEEDS, TOASTED

1 TEASPOON SESAME OIL

1 TEASPOON SHERRY

12 WONTON WRAPPERS

SEAFOOD WONTON SOUP

YIELD: **4 SERVINGS**

ACTIVE TIME: **40 MINUTES**

TOTAL TIME: **1 HOUR**

DIRECTIONS

1. In a medium saucepan, add the sesame oil and cook over medium heat until warm.

2. Add the onion and carrots and cook for 5 minutes, or until soft. Add the garlic, cook for 2 minutes, and then add the sake, fish stock, lemongrass, soy sauce, and fish sauce.

3. Simmer for 10 minutes, then remove the lemongrass and season with salt and pepper.

4. Bring the soup to a boil and add the Seafood Wontons. Reduce heat so that the soup simmers and cook for 5 minutes, or until the wontons float to the top.

5. Place 3 wontons in each bowl. Ladle the broth over the wontons, and garnish with romaine lettuce, toasted sesame seeds, cilantro, and shaved radish.

SEAFOOD WONTONS

1. Combine all ingredients, except the wonton wrappers, in a bowl and mix until combined.

2. Place 2 teaspoons of the mixture into the center of a wonton wrapper.

3. Dip your finger into cold water and rub a small amount around the edge of the wonton wrapper. Bring each corner together to make a purse and seal.

4. Repeat with remaining wonton wrappers and refrigerate until ready to use.

SOPA DE CAMARÓN SECO

YIELD: **4 SERVINGS**

ACTIVE TIME: **30 MINUTES**

TOTAL TIME: **1 HOUR**

INGREDIENTS

4 GUAJILLO CHILI PEPPERS, STEMMED AND SEEDED

2–3 DRIED CHILIS DE ARBOL, STEMMED AND SEEDED

8 OZ. DRIED SHRIMP, WITH HEADS AND TAILS

2–3 FRESH EPAZOTE LEAVES

2 TABLESPOONS LARD

1 SMALL WHITE ONION, JULIENNED

4 GARLIC CLOVES, SLICED THIN

⅛ TEASPOON DRIED MEXICAN OREGANO

1 BAY LEAF

1 CORN TORTILLA, TOASTED

SALT, TO TASTE

LIME WEDGES, FOR SERVING

DIRECTIONS

1. Place the chilis in a dry skillet and toast until fragrant and pliable. Remove the chilies from the pan and chop them.

2. Place water in a medium saucepan and bring it to a simmer. Add the dried shrimp and epazote and simmer for 10 minutes. Remove the pan from heat and let the mixture steep for 10 minutes. Strain and reserve the shrimp and the broth.

3. Place the lard in a medium saucepan and warm over medium heat. Add the onion, garlic, chiles, and half of the shrimp and cook, stirring, for 1 to 2 minutes. Add the oregano, shrimp broth, bay leaf, and tortilla and simmer for 5 to 10 minutes.

4. Remove the bay leaf and discard it. Place the soup in a blender and puree until smooth, 2 to 3 minutes. Return the mixture to the pan and simmer for 5 minutes.

5. Season the soup with salt. Divide the remaining shrimp between the serving bowls and ladle the soup into each one. Serve with lime wedges.

SOUTH INDIAN-STYLE MUTTON SOUP

YIELD: **4 TO 6 SERVINGS**

ACTIVE TIME: **30 MINUTES**

TOTAL TIME: **1 HOUR AND 15 MINUTES**

INGREDIENTS

4 TABLESPOONS VEGETABLE OIL

1½ LBS. MUTTON SHOULDER, CUT INTO ½-INCH PIECES

2 CURRY LEAVES

2 TEASPOONS BLACK PEPPERCORNS

2 TEASPOONS CUMIN SEEDS

2 TABLESPOONS FENNEL SEEDS

2 CINNAMON STICKS

4 CLOVES

4 CARDAMOM PODS, SEEDS REMOVED, SHELLS DISCARDED

2 BAY LEAVES

8 CUPS LAMB STOCK

4 SHALLOTS, PEELED AND MINCED

4 GARLIC CLOVES, MINCED

1-INCH PIECE OF GINGER, PEELED AND MINCED

2 TOMATOES, CHOPPED

½ TEASPOON TURMERIC

2 TEASPOONS GROUND CUMIN

2 TEASPOONS PAPRIKA

2 CUPS PEELED AND CHOPPED POTATOES

SALT AND PEPPER, TO TASTE

CILANTRO LEAVES, CHOPPED, FOR GARNISH

DIRECTIONS

1. In a large saucepan, add 2 tablespoons of the vegetable oil and cook over medium heat until warm.

2. Add the mutton and cook for 5 minutes, or until evenly browned.

3. Add the curry leaves, peppercorns, cumin seeds, fennel seeds, cinnamon sticks, cloves, cardamom seeds, and bay leaves and cook for 3 minutes, or until fragrant.

4. Add the stock and bring to a boil.

5. Reduce the heat so that the soup simmers and cook for 10 minutes.

6. Meanwhile, in a medium saucepan, add the remaining oil and cook over medium heat until warm.

7. Add the shallots, garlic, and ginger and cook for 3 minutes, or until fragrant.

8. Add the tomatoes, turmeric, ground cumin, and paprika, reduce the flame to low, and cook for 10 minutes, or until tomatoes are mushy.

9. Add the contents of the medium saucepan to the mutton broth and bring to a boil.

10. Reduce the heat so that the soup simmers and cook for 15 minutes. Add the potatoes and cook for 20 minutes, or until the potatoes and mutton are tender.

11. Season with salt and pepper. Serve in warmed bowls, with crusty bread, and garnish with cilantro leaves.

SPICY EGGPLANT & BEEF SOUP

YIELD: **4 SERVINGS**

ACTIVE TIME: **45 MINUTES**

TOTAL TIME: **2 HOURS AND 30 MINUTES**

DIRECTIONS

1. Soak the dried chiles in water for 30 minutes.

2. In a large saucepan, add the stock, ginger, cinnamon, star anise, peppercorns, cardamom, lime leaf, lemongrass, and galangal root. Bring to a boil, add the brisket, cover, and reduce heat so that the soup simmers. Cook for 1 hour.

3. Remove the lid and add the soy sauce and Tuk Trey.

4. Simmer for 45 minutes, uncovered, until the stock is reduced by half.

5. Remove the brisket. Skim any fat from the top, strain the stock through a fine sieve, and set aside.

6. Tear or cut the brisket into thin strips.

7. Drain the soaked chiles and finely chop, removing any seeds.

8. In a medium saucepan, add the oil and cook over medium heat until warm. Add the shallot and chopped chiles and cook for 5 minutes.

9. Add the strained broth to the saucepan and bring to a simmer.

10. Add the tamarind extract, jaggery, brisket, and eggplant. Cook for an additional 20 minutes.

11. Season the soup to taste. Stir in the curry leaves and watercress and cook for an additional 2 minutes.

12. Ladle the soup into warmed bowls, garnish with the curry leaves, chopped red chiles, and toasted peanuts and serve.

TUK TREY

1. Add all the ingredients to a mixing bowl and stir until well-combined. Place in refrigerator until ready to use.

INGREDIENTS

2 DRIED NEW MEXICO CHILES

8 CUPS VEAL OR BEEF STOCK

3-INCH PIECE OF GINGER, SLICED

1 CINNAMON STICK

2 STAR ANISE

½ TEASPOON BLACK PEPPERCORNS

4 CARDAMOM PODS, SEEDS REMOVED AND CHOPPED

1 LIME LEAF

1 LEMONGRASS STALK, BRUISED

1-INCH PIECE OF GALANGAL ROOT, CHOPPED

1 LB. BRISKET

1 TABLESPOON SOY SAUCE

3 TABLESPOONS TUK TREY (SEE RECIPE)

1 TABLESPOON VEGETABLE OIL

1 SHALLOT, FINELY CHOPPED

2 TABLESPOONS TAMARIND EXTRACT

1 TABLESPOON JAGGERY

8 THAI EGGPLANTS, STEMS REMOVED, CUT INTO ¼-INCH SLICES

1 TEASPOON CHOPPED CURRY LEAVES, PLUS MORE FOR GARNISH

½ BUNCH OF WATERCRESS

SALT AND PEPPER, TO TASTE

RED CHILIES, SEEDS REMOVED, SLICED, FOR GARNISH

TOASTED PEANUTS, FOR GARNISH

TUK TREY

1 TEASPOON SUGAR

1½ TABLESPOONS FISH SAUCE

JUICE OF ½ LIME

2 TABLESPOONS WATER

1 GARLIC CLOVE, MINCED

¼ CUP ROASTED PEANUTS, CHOPPED

½ RED CHILI, SEEDS REMOVED, FINELY CHOPPED

SPLIT PEA SOUP WITH SMOKED HAM

YIELD: **4 SERVINGS**

ACTIVE TIME: **30 MINUTES**

TOTAL TIME: **1 HOUR AND 15 MINUTES TO 2 HOURS**

INGREDIENTS

2 TABLESPOONS UNSALTED BUTTER

1 ONION, FINELY CHOPPED

1 CARROT, PEELED AND FINELY CHOPPED

1 CELERY STALK, FINELY CHOPPED

5 CUPS CHICKEN STOCK

1 CUP SPLIT PEAS

6 OZ. SMOKED HAM, CUT INTO BITE-SIZED PIECES

2 PARSLEY SPRIGS

1 BAY LEAF

1 TEASPOON CHOPPED THYME

SALT AND PEPPER, TO TASTE

PARSLEY, LEAVES REMOVED AND CHOPPED, FOR GARNISH

LEMON WEDGES, FOR GARNISH

DIRECTIONS

1. In a medium saucepan, add the butter and cook over medium heat until melted. Add the onion, carrot, and celery and cook for 5 minutes, or until soft.

2. Add the stock, peas, ham, parsley, bay leaf, and thyme. Bring to a boil, then reduce heat so that the soup simmers. Cook for 45 minutes, or until peas are cooked through. Stir occasionally as the soup cooks and add more stock if it gets too thick.

3. Discard bay leaf and parsley sprigs. Season with salt and pepper and ladle into warm bowls. Garnish with chopped parsley and serve with lemon wedges.

SWEET POTATO SOUP

YIELD: **4 TO 6 SERVINGS**

ACTIVE TIME: **25 MINUTES**

TOTAL TIME: **55 MINUTES**

INGREDIENTS

1½ TABLESPOONS UNSALTED
BUTTER

1 SMALL ONION, CHOPPED

5 CUPS CHICKEN STOCK

½ TEASPOON CURRY POWDER, PLUS
MORE FOR GARNISH

10 CUPS PEELED AND CHOPPED
SWEET POTATOES

2 TABLESPOONS MAPLE SYRUP

2 THYME SPRIGS, LEAVES REMOVED
AND CHOPPED

PINCH OF CAYENNE PEPPER

2 CUPS HEAVY CREAM

2 PINCHES GROUND NUTMEG

SALT AND PEPPER, TO TASTE

CILANTRO, FOR GARNISH

TO SERVE:

RUM CREAM

RUM CREAM

½ CUP HEAVY CREAM

¼ TEASPOON LEMON JUICE

⅛ TEASPOON LEMON ZEST

2 TABLESPOONS MYERS'S RUM

PINCH OF SUGAR

DIRECTIONS

1. In a medium saucepan, add the butter and cook over medium heat until melted. Add the onion and cook for 5 minutes, or until soft.

2. Add the chicken stock, curry powder, sweet potato, maple syrup, thyme, and cayenne pepper. Bring to a boil, reduce heat so that the soup simmers, and cook for 25 minutes, or until the sweet potatoes are soft.

3. Remove the thyme sprigs and transfer the soup to a food processor. Puree until creamy and then pass through a fine sieve.

4. Return the soup to the pan and bring to a simmer. Add the cream, nutmeg, salt, and pepper.

5. Ladle into bowls and garnish with a dollop of Rum Cream, a sprinkle of curry powder, and cilantro.

RUM CREAM

1. In a bowl, add cream and whip until medium peaks form.

2. Add the lemon juice, lemon zest, rum, and sugar. Stir to combine and refrigerate until ready to use.

INGREDIENTS

2 TABLESPOONS SESAME OIL

4 GARLIC CLOVES, MINCED

3-INCH PIECE OF GINGER, MINCED

2 TABLESPOONS CHILI BEAN SAUCE

3 CUPS CHICKEN STOCK

3 CUPS DASHI STOCK

¼ CUP SOY SAUCE

1 TABLESPOON SAKE

2 TEASPOONS SUGAR

SALT AND PEPPER, TO TASTE

NOODLES FROM 2 PACKETS OF RAMEN

SCALLION GREENS, FOR GARNISH

TO SERVE:

SZECHUAN PEPPERCORN AND CHILI OIL

CRISPY SCALLIONS

POACHED EGGS

SZECHUAN PEPPERCORN AND CHILI OIL

1½ CUPS VEGETABLE OIL

5 STAR ANISE

1 CINNAMON STICK

2 BAY LEAVES

3 TABLESPOONS SZECHUAN PEPPERCORNS

⅓ CUP RED PEPPER FLAKES

1 TEASPOON SALT

CRISPY SCALLIONS

1 CUP OIL

4 SCALLIONS, WHITE PART CUT INTO THICK MATCHSTICKS, GREENS RESERVED FOR GARNISH

SALT AND PEPPER, TO TASTE

SZECHUAN SPICED SHOYU RAMEN

YIELD: **4 SERVINGS**

ACTIVE TIME: **30 MINUTES**

TOTAL TIME: **1 HOUR AND 15 MINUTES**

DIRECTIONS

1. In a medium saucepan, add the sesame oil and warm over medium heat. Add the garlic and ginger and cook for 3 minutes, or until fragrant. Add the chili bean sauce and cook for 1 minute.

2. Add the chicken stock, dashi stock, soy sauce, and sake. Bring to a boil and then reduce heat so that the soup simmers. Cook for 5 minutes, adjust the seasoning with sugar, salt, and pepper, and turn off the heat.

3. Meanwhile, cook the ramen noodles to the manufacturer's instructions. When cooked, place in warm bowls.

4. Bring the broth to a boil and then pour over the ramen noodles. Garnish with Poached Eggs, Szechuan Peppercorn and Chili Oil, Crispy Scallions, and scallion greens.

SZECHUAN PEPPERCORN AND CHILE OIL

1. In a small saucepan, add the vegetable oil, star anise, cinnamon stick, bay leaves, and Szechuan peppercorns. Cook over the lowest-possible heat for 20 minutes, being careful not to burn.

2. Place the red pepper flakes in a small bowl. Strain the warm oil over the flakes. Let cool, season with salt, and reserve until ready to use.

CRISPY SCALLIONS

1. Place the oil in a Dutch oven and cook over medium-high heat until it reaches 350°F.

2. Bring a pot of water to boil. Add the scallion whites and cook for 2 minutes. Remove, submerge in ice water, and then dry thoroughly.

3. Place the scallion whites into the oil. Stir constantly and fry until golden brown.

4. Remove with slotted spoon or large tweezers. Set on paper towels to drain, season with salt and pepper, and serve.

TACO SOUP

YIELD: **4 SERVINGS**

ACTIVE TIME: **20 MINUTES**

TOTAL TIME: **45 MINUTES**

INGREDIENTS

2 TABLESPOONS VEGETABLE OIL

1 ONION, CHOPPED

1 RED BELL PEPPER, SEEDS REMOVED AND CHOPPED

1 GREEN BELL PEPPER, SEEDS REMOVED AND CHOPPED

1 LB. GROUND BEEF

2 TABLESPOONS TACO SEASONING

2 CUPS BEEF STOCK

2 CUPS SPAGHETTI SAUCE

2 (14 OZ.) CANS OF DICED TOMATOES

2 CUPS COOKED BLACK BEANS

2 CUPS COOKED KIDNEY BEANS

2 CUPS COOKED CORN KERNELS

½ CUP SALSA

4 CUPS TORTILLA CHIPS, FOR GARNISH

2 CUPS GRATED MONTEREY JACK CHEESE, FOR GARNISH

1 CUP SOUR CREAM, FOR GARNISH

DIRECTIONS

1. In a medium saucepan, add the oil and cook over medium heat until warm.

2. Add the onion and bell peppers and cook for 5 minutes, or until soft.

3. Add the ground beef and taco seasoning and cook for 5 minutes.

4. Add the beef stock, spaghetti sauce, and diced tomatoes and bring to a simmer. Cook for 10 minutes.

5. Add the black beans, kidney beans, and corn. Return to a simmer, add salsa, and simmer for 5 additional minutes.

6. Serve in bowls, and garnish with tortilla chips, Monterey Jack cheese, and sour cream.

YIELD: **4 SERVINGS**

ACTIVE TIME: **30 MINUTES**

TOTAL TIME: **1 HOUR**

INGREDIENTS

THAI CURRY PASTE

2 SHALLOTS, FINELY CHOPPED

2-INCH PIECE OF LEMONGRASS,
FINELY CHOPPED

1-INCH GALANGAL ROOT, GRATED

3 GARLIC CLOVES, MINCED

LOBSTER WONTONS

1½ CUPS LOBSTER MEAT, COOKED,
FINELY CHOPPED

1 SCALLION, FINELY SLICED

SALT AND PEPPER, TO TASTE

1 EGG, BEATEN

24 WONTON WRAPPERS

SOUP

1 TABLESPOON SESAME OIL

1 TABLESPOON RED THAI CURRY
PASTE

2 TEASPOONS SUGAR

3 TABLESPOONS FISH SAUCE

1 (14 OZ.) CAN COCONUT MILK

JUICE OF 1 LIME

SALT AND PEPPER, TO TASTE

THAI CHILES, SLICED, FOR
GARNISH

CILANTRO, CHOPPED, FOR
GARNISH

THAI COCONUT BROTH WITH LOBSTER WONTONS

DIRECTIONS

THAI CURRY PASTE

1. Place all ingredients in a food processor and puree until smooth. Refrigerate until ready to use.

LOBSTER WONTONS

1. Place the lobster meat, scallion, salt, and pepper in a mixing bowl, and stir to combine.

2. Place 1 tablespoon of lobster filling in the center of a wonton wrapper. Dip a finger into the egg and then rub it around the edge of the wrapper. Bring each corner of the wrapper together, and seal.

3. Repeat Step 2 with remaining wonton wrappers. When all of the wontons have been made, refrigerate until ready to use.

SOUP

1. In a medium saucepan, add the sesame oil and warm over low heat. Add the Thai curry paste and cook, while stirring constantly, for 5 minutes.

2. Meanwhile, bring 8 cups of water to boil in a large saucepan. Add the wontons and cook for 3 minutes.

3. Remove the wontons from the water with a slotted spoon and place in warm bowls.

4. Add the sugar, fish sauce, and coconut milk to the medium saucepan. Cook on low heat for 4 minutes, while stirring constantly. Season with the lime juice, salt, and pepper, while taking care not to bring to a boil.

5. Pour the soup over the wontons. Garnish with the cilantro and Thai chiles, and serve.

TOMATO ALPHABET SOUP

YIELD: **4 SERVINGS**

ACTIVE TIME: **15 MINUTES**

TOTAL TIME: **30 MINUTES**

INGREDIENTS

1 CUP ALPHABET PASTA

¼ CUP UNSALTED BUTTER

2 ONIONS, CHOPPED

4 CARROTS, CHOPPED

2 CELERY STALKS, CHOPPED

3 CUPS VEGETABLE STOCK

2 TEASPOONS CHOPPED BASIL

4 (14 OZ.) CANS DICED TOMATOES

SALT AND PEPPER, TO TASTE

DIRECTIONS

1. Cook the pasta according to the manufacturer's instructions. Drain and set aside.

2. In a medium saucepan, add the butter and cook over medium heat until melted.

3. Add the onions, carrots, and celery and cook for 5 minutes, or until soft.

4. Add the vegetable stock, basil, and tomatoes and bring to a boil.

5. Reduce heat so that the soup simmers and cook for 10 minutes.

6. Transfer soup to a food processor and puree until smooth.

7. Return to a clean pan, bring to a simmer, and add the cooked pasta. Season with salt and pepper and serve in warmed bowls.

TOMATO SOUP WITH CHICKPEAS AND PASTA

YIELD: **4 SERVINGS**

ACTIVE TIME: **20 MINUTES**

TOTAL TIME: **45 MINUTES**

INGREDIENTS

2 TABLESPOONS EXTRA-VIRGIN OLIVE OIL

1 ONION, CHOPPED

2 GARLIC CLOVES, MINCED

4 (14 OZ.) CANS STEWED TOMATOES, PUREED

2 THYME SPRIGS, LEAVES REMOVED AND CHOPPED

4 CUPS CHICKEN STOCK

½ CUP DITALINI PASTA

1 (14 OZ.) CAN CHICKPEAS, RINSED AND DRAINED

¼ CUP CHOPPED PARSLEY LEAVES

¼ CUP GRATED PARMESAN CHEESE, PLUS MORE FOR GARNISH

SALT AND PEPPER, TO TASTE

BASIL, CHOPPED, FOR GARNISH

DIRECTIONS

1. In a large saucepan, add the oil and cook over medium heat until warm.

2. Add the onion and cook for 5 minutes, or until soft. Add the garlic and cook for 2 minutes.

3. Add the pureed tomatoes, thyme, and stock and bring to a boil.

4. Reduce heat so that the soup simmers. Add the pasta and cook for 8 to 10 minutes, or until the pasta is tender.

5. Add the chickpeas, parsley, and Parmesan and cook for 3 minutes.

6. Season with salt and pepper and serve in warm bowls garnished with Parmesan and basil.

TUNISIAN SPICED BUTTERNUT SQUASH SOUP

YIELD: **12 SERVINGS**

ACTIVE TIME: **30 MINUTES**

TOTAL TIME: **2 HOURS**

INGREDIENTS

1 LARGE BUTTERNUT SQUASH

1 TEASPOON HARISSA

1 TEASPOON SEA SALT

½ TEASPOON FRESHLY GROUND PEPPER

¼ CUP FRESH LEMON JUICE

1 TABLESPOON LEMON ZEST

½ TABLESPOON LIME ZEST

2 TABLESPOONS EXTRA-VIRGIN OLIVE OIL

2 PARSNIPS, PEELED AND CUBED

3 GARLIC CLOVES, SLICED

2 TABLESPOONS AVOCADO OIL

3 SMALL SHALLOTS, DICED

2 QUARTS CHICKEN STOCK

DIRECTIONS

1. Preheat the oven to 400°F.

2. Cut the butternut squash in half, the long way; place on a foil-lined baking sheet, skin side down.

3. In a small bowl, mix together harissa, sea salt, pepper, lemon juice, lemon and lime zest, and olive oil.

4. Spread spice mixture onto the squash, evenly covering the entire inside; reserve some of the mixture to cover the parsnips and then add the parsnips to the baking sheet, along with the garlic cloves.

5. Put the baking sheet in the oven and cook for 1 hour, or until squash is fork tender.

6. While squash is roasting, heat avocado oil in a saucepan and sauté shallots until translucent.

7. When squash is finished roasting, remove and let cool for about 30 minutes.

8. Using a large metal spoon, scoop out the flesh and place it into a food processor along with the parsnips, garlic, sautéed shallots, and some stock.

9. Pulse in batches until the mixture is smooth.

10. Put the pureed mixture back into the saucepan, and heat through with stock.

11. Allow to simmer on low for 25 minutes.

12. Season to taste before serving.

TURKEY AND WILD RICE SOUP

YIELD: **4 SERVINGS**

ACTIVE TIME: **20 MINUTES**

TOTAL TIME: **1 HOUR**

INGREDIENTS

6 CUPS TURKEY STOCK

8 SCALLIONS, SLICED

½ CUP WILD RICE

4 THYME SPRIGS, LEAVES REMOVED AND CHOPPED

8 SLICES THICK-CUT BACON, CHOPPED

¼ CUP UNSALTED BUTTER

½ CUP ALL-PURPOSE FLOUR

1 CUP MILK

1 CUP HEAVY CREAM

2 CUPS COOKED AND CHOPPED TURKEY

2 TABLESPOONS SHERRY

SALT AND PEPPER, TO TASTE

EDIBLE FLOWERS, FOR GARNISH

DIRECTIONS

1. Place the stock, scallions, wild rice, and thyme in a medium saucepan. Bring to a boil, reduce heat so that the soup simmers, and cook for 35 minutes, or until the rice is tender.

2. Meanwhile, in a large saucepan, add the bacon and cook over medium heat until crispy. Remove and set aside.

3. Place the butter in the large saucepan and melt. Sprinkle the flour into the pan and cook for 2 minutes. Slowly add the milk and heavy cream, stirring to prevent any lumps from forming. Cook for 2 minutes.

4. Add the milk-and-heavy cream mixture to the rice broth and bring to a boil.

5. Reduce heat so that the soup simmers and cook for 5 minutes, or until it has thickened.

6. Add the turkey meat, sherry, salt, and pepper. Serve in warm bowls and garnish with reserved bacon and edible flowers.

TWICE-COOKED PORK BELLY & BEAN SOUP WITH BROWN BREAD CROUTONS

DIRECTIONS

PORK BELLY

1. The day before serving this recipe, preheat the oven to 300°F.

2. In a Dutch oven, combine all pork belly ingredients. Cover and cook for about 3½ hours, or until the pork belly starts to shred.

3. Place the pork belly skin side up in a shallow baking dish along with enough of the cooking liquid to cover half of the pork belly. Strain and reserve extra liquid.

4. Place parchment paper over the pork belly, top with another pan or dish that will press down on the pork belly, and refrigerate for 24 hours.

5. After 24 hours, take out the pork belly and slice to desired portion.

6. In a saucepan over medium heat, sear the portioned pork belly, starting skin side down. (Pork belly tends to pop quite a bit when searing, so be careful.)

CROUTONS

1. Preheat the oven to 400°F.

2. Cut the brown bread scraps into cubes and toss in oil and salt. Spread the cubes on a sheet pan and bake for 10 to 15 minutes, or until crisp.

SOUP

1. The day before serving this recipe, soak the beans overnight in a covered pot.

2. Rinse the soaked beans, add to a large pot, cover the beans with water, salt generously, and cook beans until tender, then drain.

3. In a large pot combine beans, tomato sauce, water, and stock, bring to a boil, and then simmer for 30 minutes.

4. Add brown sugar and apple cider vinegar and simmer for another 20 minutes. Season with salt and pepper, to taste.

5. To serve, ladle soup into a bowl and top with seared pork belly and croutons.

YIELD: **6 TO 8 SERVINGS**

ACTIVE TIME: **40 MINUTES**

TOTAL TIME: **30 HOURS**

INGREDIENTS

PORK BELLY

4 LBS. PORK BELLY

3 BAY LEAVES

3 CUPS APPLE CIDER

2 CINNAMON STICKS

2 TEASPOONS WHOLE CLOVES

1 ONION, SLICED

2 CUPS CHICKEN STOCK

3 STAR ANISE

1 TABLESPOON PEPPERCORNS

2 CARROTS, PEELED AND CHOPPED

2 CELERY STALKS, CHOPPED

CROUTONS

DAY-OLD BREAD

2 TABLESPOONS CANOLA OIL

SALT AND PEPPER, TO TASTE

SOUP

1 LB. DRY NAVY BEANS

SALT AND PEPPER, TO TASTE

1 CUP TOMATO SAUCE

1 QUART WATER

1 QUART CHICKEN OR PORK STOCK

2 TABLESPOONS BROWN SUGAR

2 TABLESPOONS APPLE CIDER
  VINEGAR

WAGON WHEEL BEEF SOUP

YIELD: **4 SERVINGS**

ACTIVE TIME: **15 MINUTES**

TOTAL TIME: **30 MINUTES**

INGREDIENTS

1 CUP WAGON WHEEL PASTA

2 TABLESPOONS VEGETABLE OIL

1 CUP ONION, CHOPPED

1 LB. GROUND BEEF

4 CUPS SPAGHETTI SAUCE

½ TEASPOON GROUND OREGANO

2 CUPS BEEF STOCK

2 CUPS KIDNEY BEANS, DRAINED
  AND COOKED

SALT AND PEPPER, TO TASTE

DIRECTIONS

1. Cook pasta according to manufacturer's instructions. Drain and set aside.

2. In a medium saucepan, add the oil and cook over medium heat until warm. Add onions and cook for 5 minutes, or until soft.

3. Add the ground beef and cook for an additional 5 minutes.

4. Add the spaghetti sauce, oregano, beef stock, and kidney beans and bring to a gentle simmer. Cook for 10 minutes.

5. Add the cooked pasta, season with salt and pepper, and serve in warmed bowls.

WALNUT SOUP WITH CHIVE & SHALLOT OIL

YIELD: **4 SERVINGS**

ACTIVE TIME: **20 MINUTES**

TOTAL TIME: **1 HOUR AND 15 MINUTES**

INGREDIENTS

3 TABLESPOONS UNSALTED BUTTER

1 TABLESPOON MINCED SHALLOT

1 CELERY STALK, FINELY CHOPPED

3 TABLESPOONS ALL-PURPOSE FLOUR

6 CUPS CHICKEN STOCK

1 BAY LEAF

1 TABLESPOON SALT

1 PINCH BLACK PEPPER

1 CUP WALNUTS, TOASTED

2 CUPS HEAVY CREAM

CHIVE AND SHALLOT OIL, FOR GARNISH

GRATED WALNUTS, FOR GARNISH

CHIVE AND SHALLOT OIL

½ CUPS VEGETABLE OIL

1 SHALLOT, MINCED

1 TABLESPOON CHIVES, CHOPPED

DIRECTIONS

1. In a large saucepan, add the butter, shallot, and celery and cook over medium heat for 3 minutes, or until soft.

2. Sprinkle in the flour and cook for 3 minutes.

3. Add the chicken stock, bay leaf, salt, pepper, and the toasted walnuts and bring to a boil.

4. Reduce heat so that the soup simmers. Add the cream and simmer for 30 minutes.

5. Remove the bay leaf. Transfer the soup to a food processor, puree until smooth, and then strain through a fine sieve.

6. Return the soup to the pan, bring to a simmer, and adjust the seasoning.

7. Serve in warm bowls and garnish with the Chive and Shallot Oil and walnuts.

CHIVE AND SHALLOT OIL

1. In a small saucepan, add the oil and cook over medium heat until warm.

2. Add the shallot and cook for 5 minutes, or until soft.

3. Remove from heat and add chives. Transfer to a container until ready to serve.

CHAPTER 4

VEGETARIAN

You'll be sure to please both the vegetarians and omnivores in your life with the vibrantly delicious recipes in this chapter.

BABY SPINACH & YOGURT SOUP

YIELD: **4 SERVINGS**

ACTIVE TIME: **20 MINUTES**

TOTAL TIME: **1 HOUR**

INGREDIENTS

2 TABLESPOONS VEGETABLE OIL

1 ONION, CHOPPED

12 CUPS BABY SPINACH

2 SCALLIONS, CHOPPED

3 TABLESPOONS LONG-GRAIN RICE

3 CUPS VEGETABLE STOCK

1 GARLIC CLOVE, MINCED

1½ CUPS WHOLE MILK YOGURT

SALT AND PEPPER, TO TASTE

TO SERVE:

SHALLOT WILTED SPINACH

TURMERIC OIL

SHALLOT WILTED SPINACH

¼ CUP EXTRA-VIRGIN OLIVE OIL

2 SHALLOTS, MINCED

4 CUPS BABY SPINACH, PACKED

SALT AND PEPPER, TO TASTE

TURMERIC OIL

½ CUP EXTRA-VIRGIN OLIVE OIL

2 TEASPOONS TURMERIC

SALT AND PEPPER, TO TASTE

DIRECTIONS

1. In a large saucepan, add the oil and cook over medium heat until warm. Add the onion and cook for 5 minutes, or until soft.

2. Add 8 cups of the spinach, cover, and cook for 5 minutes, or until all the spinach is wilted.

3. Add the scallions, rice, and vegetable stock, and simmer for 18 minutes, or until the rice is cooked.

4. Transfer the soup to a food processor, add the garlic and remaining spinach, and puree until smooth. Strain through a fine sieve, return to a clean pan, bring to a simmer, and add yogurt.

5. Season with salt and pepper, ladle into warm bowls, and serve with Shallot Wilted Spinach and Turmeric Oil.

SHALLOT WILTED SPINACH

1. In a saucepan, add the oil and warm over medium heat. Add the shallots and cook for 3 minutes, or until soft.

2. Add the spinach and cook for 5 minutes, or until wilted.

3. Season with salt and pepper and serve.

TURMERIC OIL

1. Combine the olive oil and turmeric in a bowl and whisk vigorously.

2. Season with salt and pepper, strain through a fine sieve, and reserve until ready to use.

CARROT & GINGER SOUP WITH TURMERIC CREAM

YIELD: **4 TO 6 SERVINGS**

ACTIVE TIME: **25 MINUTES**

TOTAL TIME: **1 HOUR**

INGREDIENTS

4 TABLESPOONS UNSALTED BUTTER

2 ONIONS, DICED

6 CUPS CHOPPED CARROTS

4 TABLESPOONS PEELED AND
MINCED GINGER

ZEST AND JUICE OF 2 ORANGES

1 CUP WHITE WINE

8 CUPS CHICKEN STOCK OR
VEGETABLE STOCK

SALT AND PEPPER, TO TASTE

DILL, CHOPPED, FOR GARNISH

TO SERVE:

TURMERIC CREAM

TURMERIC CREAM

½ CUP HEAVY CREAM

½ TEASPOON TURMERIC

PINCH OF SALT

DIRECTIONS

1. In a medium saucepan, add the butter and cook over medium heat until melted. Add the onion and cook for 5 minutes, while stirring often, or until it is soft.

2. Add the carrots, ginger, and orange zest. Cook for 5 minutes, or until the carrot starts to break down.

3. Add the orange juice and white wine and cook until evaporated. Add the stock, bring to a boil, and season with salt and pepper. Reduce heat so that the soup simmers and cook for 10 to 15 minutes, until the vegetables are tender.

4. Transfer the soup to a food processor, puree until smooth, and strain through a fine sieve.

5. Return the soup to a clean pan and adjust the seasoning. Add more stock or juice if it is too thick.

6. Ladle into warm bowls, serve with Turmeric Cream, and garnish with dill.

TURMERIC CREAM

1. Place the cream in a bowl and whip until medium peaks begin to form.

2. Add the turmeric and season with salt. Stir to combine, and refrigerate until ready to use.

YIELD: **4 SERVINGS**

ACTIVE TIME: **30 MINUTES**

TOTAL TIME: **2 HOURS AND 15 MINUTES**

INGREDIENTS

8 EARS SWEET CORN

10 CUPS WATER

1 BAY LEAF

12 THYME SPRIGS

6 PEPPERCORNS

2 ONIONS, PEELED AND CHOPPED

2 TABLESPOONS UNSALTED BUTTER

4 GARLIC CLOVES, MINCED

2 TABLESPOONS LEMON JUICE

SALT AND PEPPER, TO TASTE

CILANTRO, FOR GARNISH

TO SERVE:

GARLIC CUSTARD

GARLIC CUSTARD

1 TABLESPOON UNSALTED BUTTER

3 GARLIC CLOVES, MINCED

1 CUP HEAVY CREAM

½ TEASPOON SALT

PEPPER, TO TASTE

2 MEDIUM EGGS

YOLK FROM 1 MEDIUM EGG

1½ TEASPOONS CHIVES, CHOPPED

CHILLED CORN SOUP WITH GARLIC CUSTARD

DIRECTIONS

1. Remove the corn kernels from the cobs.

2. In a large stockpot, add the water, the corn cobs, bay leaf, thyme, peppercorns, and 1 of the chopped onions, and bring to a boil.

3. Reduce the heat so that the stock simmers and cook for 1 hour.

4. Strain through a fine sieve and reserve the stock.

5. In a medium saucepan, melt the butter. Add the remaining onion and the garlic, and cook over medium heat for 5 minutes, or until soft.

6. Add the corn kernels, while reserving 2 tablespoons for garnish, and reduce the heat to low. Cook for 5 minutes.

7. Transfer the corn mixture to a food processor and combine with 4 cups of the corn stock. Puree, adding more stock if necessary to produce a creamy consistency.

8. Season with lemon juice, salt, and pepper. Chill in refrigerator for at least 1 hour.

9. Place the Garlic Custard, reserved corn kernels, and cilantro leaves in the middle of chilled bowls. Pour the soup around the center and serve.

GARLIC CUSTARD

1. Preheat the oven to 325°F.

2. Grease four 4 oz. ramekins. Place them in a baking pan.

3. In a small saucepan, melt the butter. Add the garlic and cook over low heat for 5 minutes, or until soft.

4. Add the cream and the salt. Increase heat to medium and bring to a simmer.

5. Remove from heat, let stand for 10 minutes, and strain through a fine sieve.

6. Add the eggs and the yolk to a medium-sized bowl and whisk until combined. Add chives and whisk until combined.

7. Add the garlic mixture and whisk until combined. Season with additional salt and pepper, if necessary.

8. Divide the mixture between the ramekins and place the pan in the oven. Before closing the door, pour enough hot water in the baking pan to go halfway up the ramekins.

9. Cook for 18 minutes, or until the custard is firm and a knife comes out clean when inserted.

10. Remove the pan from the oven and chill the custard in the refrigerator for 1 hour.

11. When ready to serve, use a knife to remove the custard from the ramekin.

CHILLED PEA SOUP

YIELD: **4 TO 6 SERVINGS**

ACTIVE TIME: **15 MINUTES**

TOTAL TIME: **1 HOUR AND 15 MINUTES**

INGREDIENTS

1 TABLESPOON EXTRA-VIRGIN OLIVE OIL

½ ONION, PEELED AND DICED

1 MINT SPRIG

4 CUPS VEGETABLE STOCK

3 LBS. PEAS, FROZEN

4 CUPS SPINACH

SALT AND PEPPER, TO TASTE

TO SERVE:

CHEESE GOUGERES

CHEESE GOUGERES

¾ CUP MILK

¾ CUP WATER

⅛ TEASPOON SALT

7 TABLESPOONS UNSALTED BUTTER

1¼ CUPS ALL-PURPOSE FLOUR

5 EGGS, PLUS 1 EGG FOR EGG WASH

1¼ CUPS GRATED GRUYÈRE CHEESE

DIRECTIONS

1. In a medium saucepan, add the oil and onions and cook over medium heat for 5 minutes, or until the onions are soft.

2. Add the mint sprig and stir.

3. After 1 minute, add the stock and bring to a boil. Remove from heat and add the frozen peas.

4. Transfer the soup to a food processor, add the spinach, and puree until smooth.

5. Strain through a fine sieve, season with salt and pepper, and serve with Cheese Gougeres.

CHEESE GOUGERES

1. Preheat the oven to 400°F.

2. In a medium saucepan, add the milk, water, salt, and butter and bring to a boil. Add the flour and stir constantly until a ball of dough forms.

3. Remove dough from pan and place in a stand mixer. Mix slowly until dough stops steaming.

4. Add the 5 eggs one at a time. Add the cheese and mix until combined.

5. Line a baking tray with a baking mat or parchment paper and spoon the dough onto it.

6. In a small bowl, add the remaining egg and 2 tablespoons of water and whisk until combined. Brush this wash on top of dough and place tray in oven. Bake for 20 minutes, or until golden brown, then remove and let cool on a wire rack.

COCONUT & SPINACH SOUP WITH TOASTED SLICED ALMONDS

YIELD: **4 SERVINGS**

ACTIVE TIME: **20 MINUTES**

TOTAL TIME: **45 MINUTES**

INGREDIENTS

3 TABLESPOONS UNSALTED BUTTER

1 ONION, CHOPPED

16 CUPS CHOPPED SPINACH

4 CUPS VEGETABLE STOCK

1 TABLESPOON ALL-PURPOSE FLOUR

2 CUPS COCONUT MILK

SALT AND PEPPER, TO TASTE

¼ TEASPOON NUTMEG, PLUS MORE
    FOR GARNISH

CHIVES, CHOPPED, FOR GARNISH

ALMONDS, SLICED AND TOASTED,
    FOR GARNISH

UNSWEETENED COCONUT,
    SHREDDED, FOR GARNISH

DIRECTIONS

1. Place 2 tablespoons of the butter in a medium saucepan and cook over medium heat until melted. Add the onion and cook for 5 minutes, or until soft.

2. Add the spinach, cover, and cook over low heat for 5 minutes, or until wilted.

3. Add the stock and bring to a boil.

4. Transfer the soup to a food processor, blend until creamy, and strain through a fine sieve.

5. In a clean medium saucepan, add the remaining butter and melt. Add the flour and cook for 2 minutes. Add the soup and coconut milk to the pan with the butter and flour. Cook for 5 minutes. Season with salt, pepper, and nutmeg, ladle into warm bowls, and garnish with nutmeg, chives, toasted sliced almonds, and coconut.

CREAM OF CAULIFLOWER WITH CURRIED CAULIFLOWER FLORETS

DIRECTIONS

1. Remove the florets from the stem of the cauliflower. Reserve 2 large florets and then chop the remaining florets and stem.

2. In a medium saucepan, add the butter and olive oil and cook over medium heat until warm.

3. Add the onion and chopped cauliflower and cook for 5 minutes, or until soft.

4. Add the herbs and cook for 3 minutes. Add the wine and the stock, bring to a boil, reduce heat so that the soup simmers, and cook for 5 minutes.

5. Add the cream and simmer for 20 minutes, or until the cauliflower is tender.

6. Transfer the soup to a food processor, puree until creamy, and strain through a fine sieve.

7. Return to a clean pan, bring to a simmer, and season with salt and pepper.

8. Ladle into warm bowls, serve with Curried Cauliflower Florets, and garnish with toasted almonds and pea tendrils.

CURRIED CAULIFLOWER FLORETS

1. Add 1 tablespoon of the oil to a medium saucepan and warm over medium heat.

2. Add the cauliflower and cook for 2 minutes on both sides.

3. Meanwhile, place the remaining oil and the spices in a bowl. Whisk until combined.

4. Add the spiced oil to the pan and bring to a simmer.

5. Remove from heat and let cool. Season with salt and pepper, and serve.

YIELD: **4 SERVINGS**

ACTIVE TIME: **15 MINUTES**

TOTAL TIME: **45 MINUTES**

INGREDIENTS

1 HEAD CAULIFLOWER

2 TABLESPOONS BUTTER

1 TABLESPOON EXTRA-VIRGIN
OLIVE OIL

½ ONION, DICED

1 THYME SPRIG, LEAVES REMOVED
AND CHOPPED

1 ROSEMARY SPRIG, LEAVES
REMOVED AND CHOPPED

1 CUP CHARDONNAY

1 CUP CHICKEN OR VEGETABLE
STOCK

2 CUPS HEAVY CREAM

SALT AND PEPPER, TO TASTE

ALMONDS, SLICED AND TOASTED,
FOR GARNISH

PEA TENDRILS, FOR GARNISH

TO SERVE:
CURRIED CAULIFLOWER FLORETS

CURRIED CAULIFLOWER FLORETS

½ CUP EXTRA-VIRGIN OLIVE OIL

2 LARGE CAULIFLOWER FLORETS,
SLICED INTO 8 ¼-INCH PIECES

1 TABLESPOON CURRY POWDER

⅛ TEASPOON CAYENNE PEPPER

SALT AND PEPPER, TO TASTE

CURRIED YOGURT SOUP

YIELD: **4 SERVINGS**

ACTIVE TIME: **25 MINUTES**

TOTAL TIME: **1 HOUR**

INGREDIENTS

4 CUPS PLAIN YOGURT, PLUS MORE
    FOR SERVING

½ CUP CHICKPEA FLOUR

1 TEASPOON CHILI POWDER

1 TEASPOON TURMERIC

½ TEASPOON CHOPPED JALAPEÑO

1 CUP VEGETABLE STOCK

½ CUP VEGETABLE OIL

1 DRIED RED CHILI

1 TEASPOON CUMIN

2 TEASPOONS CHOPPED DRIED
    CURRY LEAVES

6 GARLIC CLOVES, CRUSHED

2-INCH PIECE OF GINGER, PEELED
AND CRUSHED

4 TABLESPOONS CHOPPED
    CILANTRO

1 TEASPOON SUGAR

SALT AND PEPPER, TO TASTE

TO SERVE:

DRIED CILANTRO LEAVES

DRIED CILANTRO LEAVES

¼ TEASPOON OLIVE OIL

12 LARGE CILANTRO LEAVES

DIRECTIONS

1. Combine the yogurt, chickpea flour, chili powder, and turmeric in a bowl. Transfer to a saucepan, add the jalapeños and vegetable stock, and bring to a simmer. Cook for approximately 10 minutes, while stirring occasionally, taking care not to let the soup boil over.

2. Heat the vegetable oil in a sauté pan. Add the remaining spices, garlic, and ginger and cook until the dried curry turns black. Stir in the cilantro and sugar and then add the contents of the sauté pan to the soup. Cover and let stand for 10 minutes.

3. Strain the soup through a fine sieve and adjust seasoning to taste.

4. Serve in bowls with Dried Cilantro Leaves and yogurt.

DRIED CILANTRO LEAVES

1. Tightly wrap a plate with plastic wrap and then sprinkle with oil.

2. Use a paper towel to spread the oil into an even layer on the plastic wrap. Lay the leaves on the plate and cover tightly with more plastic wrap.

3. Microwave for 4 to 5 minutes, until crispy. Remove from microwave and serve.

EGGPLANT & ZUCCHINI SOUP WITH TZATZIKI, MINT-PICKLED CUCUMBERS, AND PITA BREAD

DIRECTIONS

1. Preheat the oven to 425°F.

2. Place the eggplant, zucchini, onion, and garlic in a roasting pan and drizzle with olive oil.

3. Place in the oven and roast for 30 minutes, stirring occasionally. Remove and let stand.

4. Place half of the vegetables in a food processor. Add the stock and blend until smooth.

5. Add the puree to a medium saucepan. Add the remaining vegetables and bring to a boil.

6. Stir in oregano and mint, and season with salt and pepper. Ladle into bowls, garnish with fresh mint sprigs, and serve with a scoop of Tzatziki, the Mint-Pickled Cucumbers, and Pita Bread.

TZATZIKI

1. Place the cucumber in a bowl. Sprinkle the salt over it and let stand for 20 minutes.

2. Combine the salted cucumber with the remaining ingredients. Season to taste and place in the refrigerator until ready to use.

MINT-PICKLED CUCUMBERS

1. Place all ingredients, except the cucumber, in a small saucepan and bring to a boil.

2. Turn off heat and let cool.

3. Strain through a fine sieve. Place cucumbers in the pickling liquid and marinate for 30 minutes.

YIELD: **4 SERVINGS**

ACTIVE TIME: **1 HOUR**

TOTAL TIME: **2 HOURS AND 30 MINUTES**

INGREDIENTS

1 LARGE EGGPLANT, PEELED AND DICED

2 LARGE ZUCCHINI, DICED

1 ONION, DICED

3 GARLIC CLOVES, MINCED

2 TABLESPOONS EXTRA-VIRGIN OLIVE OIL

3 CUPS VEGETABLE STOCK

1 TABLESPOON OREGANO, LEAVES REMOVED AND CHOPPED

1 TABLESPOON MINT, LEAVES REMOVED AND CHOPPED, PLUS MORE FOR GARNISH

SALT AND PEPPER, TO TASTE

TO SERVE:

TZATZIKI

PITA BREAD (SEE PAGE 342)

MINT-PICKLED CUCUMBERS

TZATZIKI

½ CUCUMBER, PEELED, SEEDS REMOVED, DICED

½ TEASPOON SALT

1 GARLIC CLOVE, MINCED

½ CUP GREEK YOGURT

2 TABLESPOONS MINT, CHOPPED

MINT-PICKLED CUCUMBERS

⅓ CUP SUGAR

⅓ CUP WATER

⅓ CUP RICE WINE VINEGAR

1 TABLESPOON DRIED MINT

1 TEASPOON CORIANDER SEEDS

1 TEASPOON MUSTARD SEEDS

½ CUCUMBER, PEELED, SEEDED, SLICED INTO HALF-MOONS

VEGETARIAN GREEN GUMBO

YIELD: **4 TO 6 SERVINGS**

ACTIVE TIME: **30 MINUTES**

TOTAL TIME: **1 HOUR**

INGREDIENTS

1 TABLESPOON VEGETABLE OIL

1 ONION, CHOPPED

2 GARLIC CLOVES, MINCED

1 CELERY STALK, FINELY CHOPPED

1 GREEN BELL PEPPER, CHOPPED

¼ GREEN CABBAGE, CORE REMOVED AND FINELY SLICED

½ TEASPOON CHOPPED OREGANO LEAVES

½ TEASPOON CHOPPED THYME LEAVES

1 BAY LEAF

6 CUPS VEGETABLE STOCK

2 CUPS FINELY SHREDDED COLLARD GREENS

2 CUPS FINELY SHREDDED SPINACH

1 BUNCH WATERCRESS

12 OZ. TOFU, CUT INTO ¼-INCH PIECES

¼ CUP CHOPPED PARSLEY LEAVES

½ TEASPOON ALLSPICE

PINCH OF CAYENNE PEPPER

SALT AND PEPPER, TO TASTE

DIRECTIONS

1. In a large saucepan, add the oil and cook over medium heat until warm.

2. Add the onions, garlic, celery, and bell pepper and cook for 5 minutes, or until soft.

3. Add the cabbage, oregano, thyme, and bay leaf and cook for 5 minutes.

4. Add the stock and bring to a boil. Reduce heat so that the soup simmers and cook for 5 minutes.

5. Add the collard greens and cook for 5 minutes, then add the spinach, watercress, and tofu. Cook for 2 minutes before adding the parsley, allspice, and cayenne. Season with salt and pepper, simmer for 2 minutes, and then serve in warm bowls.

INDO-CHINESE VEGETABLE HOT AND SOUR SOUP

YIELD: **4 SERVINGS**

ACTIVE TIME: **30 MINUTES**

TOTAL TIME: **45 MINUTES**

INGREDIENTS

3 TABLESPOONS CORNSTARCH

1 CUP WATER

1 TABLESPOON SESAME OIL

½ CUP FINELY CHOPPED ONION

2 TEASPOONS MINCED GINGER

2 TEASPOONS MINCED GARLIC

2 TABLESPOONS FINELY CHOPPED CELERY

¼ CUP FINELY SLICED GREEN BEANS

¼ CUP FINELY CHOPPED CARROT

¼ CUP FINELY CHOPPED MUSHROOMS

½ CUP FINELY SLICED GREEN CABBAGE

¼ CUP FINELY CHOPPED GREEN BELL PEPPER

4 CUPS VEGETABLE STOCK

3 TABLESPOONS SOY SAUCE

1 TEASPOON WHITE DISTILLED VINEGAR

SALT AND PEPPER, TO TASTE

BEAN SPROUTS, FOR GARNISH

2 SCALLIONS, FINELY SLICED, FOR GARNISH

DIRECTIONS

1. Place the cornstarch and the water in a bowl. Stir until cornstarch dissolves and set aside.

2. In a medium saucepan, add the oil and warm over medium heat. Add the onion, ginger, garlic, and celery and cook for 5 minutes, or until soft.

3. Add the green beans, carrot, mushrooms, cabbage, and bell pepper. Sauté for 1 minute, add the stock, and bring to a boil.

4. Reduce to a simmer and add soy sauce and vinegar.

5. Slowly add the dissolved cornstarch to the soup, whisking constantly until combined. Simmer for 5 minutes, or until thickened, stirring often.

6. Season with salt and pepper, ladle into warm bowls, and garnish with bean sprouts and scallions.

INGREDIENTS

24 OZ. CHICKPEAS

1 YELLOW BELL PEPPER, DESEEDED

6 GARLIC CLOVES, SLICED

2 ONIONS, DICED

2 CELERY STALKS, DICED

2 CARROTS, DICED

2 BAY LEAVES

4 TABLESPOONS RICE WINE VINEGAR

2 TABLESPOONS AJI-MIRIN

1 CUP MIX OF CHOPPED FRESH TARRAGON, PARSLEY, CHIVES, AND CILANTRO

3 TABLESPOONS SESAME OIL

3 TABLESPOONS EXTRA-VIRGIN OLIVE OIL

2 TABLESPOONS SRIRACHA

2 TEASPOONS TURMERIC

4 TABLESPOONS SALT, DIVIDED

4 TABLESPOONS BLACK PEPPER, DIVIDED

2 GALLONS CORN STOCK OR VEGETABLE STOCK

1 CUP TOMATO CONCASSE (SEE PAGE 339), SPIKED WITH CILANTRO

¼ CUP FRESH LIME JUICE

1 TABLESPOON BERBERE SPICE MIX (SEE RECIPE)

1 DOLLOP CRÈME FRAÎCHE, FOR GARNISH

1 SPRIG DILL, FOR GARNISH (OPTIONAL)

CAVIAR, FOR GARNISH (OPTIONAL)

BERBERE SPICE MIX

1 CUP HOT PAPRIKA OR CHILI POWDER

½ TABLESPOON GROUND CLOVES

1 TABLESPOON GROUND CARDAMOM

1 TABLESPOON GINGER POWDER

1 TABLESPOON ONION POWDER

1 TABLESPOON CORIANDER

1 TABLESPOON CUMIN

½ TABLESPOON CINNAMON

½ TABLESPOON GROUND NUTMEG

½ TABLESPOON GROUND FENUGREEK SEEDS

1 TABLESPOON BLACK PEPPER

1 TABLESPOON SEA SALT

ISRAELI SPICY CHICKPEA SOUP WITH CRÈME FRAÎCHE

YIELD: **12 SERVINGS**

ACTIVE TIME: **15 MINUTES**

TOTAL TIME: **45 MINUTES**

DIRECTIONS

1. Combine all of the ingredients, except the stock, tomato concasse, lime juice, and Berbere Spice Mix, in a large pot and sauté for 10 minutes, adding the salt and pepper in stages to layer the flavor.

2. Add the stock and bring to a simmer and cook for 20 minutes, seasoning again with salt and pepper.

3. Using a slotted spoon, reserve 2 cups of the cooked vegetables from the soup for garnish and mix them with the tomato concasse.

4. Place the rest of the ingredients in a blender and blend until thick and smooth. Adjust seasoning with lime juice and Berbere Spice Mix.

5. Pass through a fine mesh sieve to get rid of any chunky vegetables. The soup should have a velvety smooth and silky texture with a beautiful golden color.

6. To serve, garnish with reserved ingredients and a dollop of crème fraîche, and if desired dill and caviar.

BERBERE SPICE MIX

1. Sift all of the spices into a bowl, mix well, and set aside.

MISO BROTH WITH FRIED TOFU

YIELD: **4 SERVINGS**

ACTIVE TIME: **30 MINUTES**

TOTAL TIME: **1 HOUR**

DIRECTIONS

1. In a stockpot, add the scallion greens, cilantro stalks, ginger, star anise, cinnamon stick, cardamom seeds, bay leaf, red pepper flakes, and dashi stock. Cook over medium heat until boiling, reduce the heat, and simmer for 10 minutes.

2. Strain the broth through a fine sieve. Return to the stockpot and bring to a simmer.

3. Add the bok choy and cook for 5 minutes. Add the scallion whites and cook for an additional 2 minutes.

4. Place the miso in a small bowl, add a bit of the hot stock, and then place in the soup.

5. Add soy sauce. Ladle into warm bowls, garnish with the cilantro and Thai chili, and serve with Fried Tofu and Crispy Wonton Skins.

FRIED TOFU

1. Place oil in a medium saucepan and heat to 350°F.

2. Place the eggs, flour, and panko bread crumbs in 3 separate bowls.

3. Dredge the tofu in the flour, remove, and shake to remove any excess flour. Place the coated tofu in the egg wash. Remove from egg wash, shake to release any excess egg, and gently coat with bread crumbs.

4. If there is any tofu exposed, return to the egg mix and repeat with bread crumbs.

5. Once all the tofu is coated, place in oil and fry in batches until golden brown. Remove with a slotted spoon, place on a paper towel, and season with salt.

6. Reduce the heat of the oil to 300°F and reserve for the Crispy Wonton Skins.

CRISPY WONTON SKINS

1. Place the wonton wrappers in the reserved oil and turn frequently until they are crisp and golden brown.

2. Use a slotted spoon to remove the fried wonton wrappers from oil and set on paper towels to drain.

3. Season with salt, and serve.

INGREDIENTS

4 SCALLIONS, WHITES SLICED THIN, GREENS RESERVED FOR BROTH

4 CILANTRO SPRIGS, LEAVES RESERVED FOR GARNISH, STALKS RESERVED FOR BROTH

1-INCH PIECE OF GINGER, SLICED

1 STAR ANISE

1 CINNAMON STICK

4 CARDAMOM PODS, SEEDS REMOVED FROM SHELL AND CRUSHED

1 BAY LEAF

½ TEASPOON RED PEPPER FLAKES

4 CUPS OF DASHI STOCK

3 BOK CHOY, CUT LENGTHWISE INTO EIGHTHS

¼ CUP RED MISO

2 TABLESPOONS SOY SAUCE

THAI CHILI, SEEDS REMOVED, THINLY SLICED, FOR GARNISH

TO SERVE:

FRIED TOFU

CRISPY WONTON SKINS

FRIED TOFU

2 CUPS VEGETABLE OIL

2 EGGS, WHISKED TOGETHER

¼ CUP FLOUR

1 ½ CUPS PANKO, GROUND TO A FINE POWDER IN FOOD PROCESSOR

5 OZ. TOFU, CUT INTO ¾-INCH CUBES, DRIED ON A PAPER TOWEL

SALT, TO TASTE

CRISPY WONTON SKINS

4 WONTON WRAPPERS, CUT INTO TRIANGLES

SALT, TO TASTE

POTAGE OF LENTILS WITH CONFIT LEMON RINDS

YIELD: **4 TO 6 SERVINGS**

ACTIVE TIME: **30 MINUTES**

TOTAL TIME: **1 HOUR**

INGREDIENTS

¼ CUP LEMON OIL (SEE CONFIT LEMON RINDS RECIPE)

1 ONION, FINELY CHOPPED

2 CELERY STALKS, FINELY CHOPPED

2 CARROTS, PEELED AND FINELY CHOPPED

4 GARLIC CLOVES, MINCED

1 POTATO, PEELED AND DICED

1 CUP RED LENTILS, RINSED

6 CUPS VEGETABLE STOCK

1 BAY LEAF

2 TABLESPOONS LEMON JUICE

½ TEASPOON CUMIN

½ TEASPOON TABASCO

SALT AND PEPPER, TO TASTE

PARSLEY, CHOPPED, FOR GARNISH

TO SERVE:

CONFIT LEMON RINDS

CONFIT LEMON RINDS

1 LEMON, PEELED AND THINLY SLICED, JUICE RESERVED FOR SOUP

½ CUP EXTRA-VIRGIN OLIVE OIL

DIRECTIONS

1. In a medium saucepan, add the lemon oil and cook over medium heat until warm. Add the onion and cook for 4 to 5 minutes, or until soft.

2. Add the celery, carrots, garlic, and potato, and continue until the vegetables begin to soften.

3. Add the lentils, 4 cups of the stock, bay leaf, lemon juice, cumin, and Tabasco and bring to a boil. Reduce the heat and simmer for 10 minutes, or until the potato and lentils are tender.

4. Remove the bay leaf and use a slotted spoon to remove ½ cup of the solids from the soup. Set aside and use for garnish. Transfer the rest of the soup to a food processor and puree until smooth.

5. Return to the pan, add the remaining stock, and season with salt and pepper. Ladle into bowls, garnish with parsley and reserved lentils and vegetables, and serve with Confit Lemon Rinds.

CONFIT LEMON RINDS

1. Add the lemon peel and oil to a small saucepan, bring to a simmer, and cook for 10 minutes.

2. Turn off the heat and let cool. Strain oil and use in the soup. Reserve lemon rind until ready to serve.

ROASTED PUMPKIN MOLE SOUP

YIELD: **4 SERVINGS**

ACTIVE TIME: **20 MINUTES**

TOTAL TIME: **1 HOUR AND 30 MINUTES**

INGREDIENTS

1½ TABLESPOONS EXTRA-VIRGIN OLIVE OIL

1 (3 LBS.) PUMPKIN, HALVED, SEEDS REMOVED

½ CUP PUMPKIN SEEDS

1 TEASPOON BROWN SUGAR

½ TEASPOON CUMIN

¼ TEASPOON SALT

1 ANCHO CHILI, SOAKED IN WARM WATER FOR 20 MINUTES, DRAINED, EXCESS WATER SQUEEZED OUT

1 TABLESPOON MOLE PASTE

¼ CUP WATER

2 CUPS BUTTERMILK

SALT AND PEPPER, TO TASTE

CHIVES, CHOPPED, FOR GARNISH

TO SERVE:

LIME SOUR CREAM

LIME SOUR CREAM

1 CUP SOUR CREAM

ZEST AND JUICE OF 1 LIME

SALT AND PEPPER, TO TASTE

DIRECTIONS

1. Preheat the oven to 450°F.

2. Sprinkle 1 tablespoon of the olive oil on a baking tray. Place the two pumpkin halves on the tray, flesh side down, and bake for 30 minutes, or until the flesh is tender.

3. Remove from the oven and let stand for 30 minutes.

4. Meanwhile, reduce the oven temperature to 325°F.

5. Place the pumpkin seeds, brown sugar, cumin, salt, and remaining olive oil in a bowl. Toss until the seeds are coated, place on a baking tray, and bake for 8 minutes. Remove from oven and set aside.

6. Scoop the flesh out of the cooked pumpkin and place in a food processor with the ancho chili. Puree until smooth.

7. In a small saucepan, add the mole paste and water. Cook over low heat and whisk until it forms a thick paste. Remove from heat and set aside.

8. In a large saucepan, add the pumpkin puree, the mole sauce, and the buttermilk. Bring to a simmer, while stirring constantly. Season with salt and pepper and ladle into warm bowls. Garnish with chives, toasted pumpkin seeds, and Lime Sour Cream.

LIME SOUR CREAM

1. Place all of the ingredients in a bowl and stir until combined. Refrigerate until ready to use.

INGREDIENTS

4 CUPS VEGETABLE STOCK

1¼ CUPS DRIED SHIITAKE
  MUSHROOMS

3 LARGE DRIED PASILLA PEPPERS,
  STEMS AND SEEDS REMOVED

1 LEMONGRASS STALK, FINELY
  SLICED

½ TEASPOON GROUND TURMERIC

1 TABLESPOON GRATED GALANGAL
  ROOT

1 ONION, CHOPPED

½ TABLESPOON SHRIMP PASTE

1 TABLESPOON VEGETABLE OIL

1 TABLESPOON TAMARIND PASTE

1 TABLESPOON JAGGERY

SALT AND PEPPER, TO TASTE

3 OZ. RICE NOODLES

SMALL CUCUMBER, SEEDED, CUT
  INTO THIN STRIPS, FOR GARNISH

FRESH MINT LEAVES, FOR GARNISH

TO SERVE:

CRISPY RED ONION RINGS

CRISPY RED ONION RINGS

1 SMALL RED ONION, PEELED AND
  FINELY SLICED INTO RINGS

1 CUP BUTTERMILK

2 CUPS VEGETABLE OIL

½ CUP ALL-PURPOSE FLOUR

½ CUP CORNSTARCH

SALT AND PEPPER, TO TASTE

SHIITAKE MUSHROOM LAKSA

YIELD: **4 SERVINGS**

ACTIVE TIME: **30 MINUTES**

TOTAL TIME: **1 HOUR AND 30 MINUTES**

DIRECTIONS

1. In a medium saucepan, add the vegetable stock and bring to a boil.

2. Pour the boiling stock over the dried shiitakes and let soak for 20 minutes. Strain and reserve the liquid.

3. Place the dried Pasilla peppers in a small bowl, cover with hot water, and soak for 5 minutes. Strain and reserve the liquid.

4. In a food processor, add the lemongrass, turmeric, galangal, onion, soaked Pasilla peppers, and shrimp paste. Add a bit of the Pasilla soaking water and blend to form a paste.

5. In a saucepan, add the oil and cook over low heat until warm. Add the paste and cook for 5 minutes, or until fragrant.

6. Add the tamarind paste, mushroom liquid, and jaggery. Simmer for 25 minutes.

7. Strain the soup and return the broth to a pan. Add the soaked shiitakes, return to a simmer, and season with salt and pepper.

8. Place the rice noodles in a bowl and cover with boiling water. Let soak for 4 minutes, or according to the manufacturer's instructions.

9. Place the noodles in hot bowls and ladle the soup over the top. Garnish with cucumber, mint, and Crispy Red Onion Rings.

CRISPY RED ONION RINGS

1. Place the red onion and buttermilk in a bowl and soak for 30 minutes.

2. Meanwhile, place the oil in a Dutch oven and heat to 375°F.

3. Combine the flour and cornstarch and pass through a fine sieve.

4. Dredge the marinated onions in the dry mixture until they are nicely coated.

5. Drop the onions into the hot oil one at a time and fry until golden brown.

6. Remove from oil, set to drain on a paper towel, and season with salt and pepper.

SIMPLE BLACK BEAN SOUP

YIELD: **4 TO 6 SERVINGS**

ACTIVE TIME: **10 MINUTES**

TOTAL TIME: **16 HOURS**

INGREDIENTS

1 LB. DRIED BLACK BEANS

1 MEDIUM WHITE OR YELLOW ONION, DICED

¼ CUP CHOPPED CILANTRO

1–2 BAY LEAVES

1 TABLESPOON SALT

2 TABLESPOONS CUMIN

5 GARLIC CLOVES, MINCED

4 CUPS WATER

1 JALAPEÑO PEPPER, SLICED, FOR GARNISH

CILANTRO, CHOPPED, FOR GARNISH

1 RADISH, SLICED, FOR GARNISH

HOT SAUCE, FOR GARNISH

CHEDDAR CHEESE, SHREDDED, FOR GARNISH

LIME WEDGES, FOR GARNISH

DIRECTIONS

1. Place the black beans in a container and cover with 1 inch of water. Let soak overnight. Once soaked, drain off the liquid and rinse the beans before putting them in a slow cooker.

2. Add the remaining ingredients to the slow cooker and cook on low for 4 hours.

3. After 4 hours, check the beans. If you are able to mash them with your fingers, they are done.

4. Garnish and serve.

SOPA DE FLOR DE CALABAZA

YIELD: **4 SERVINGS**

ACTIVE TIME: **30 MINUTES**

TOTAL TIME: **30 MINUTES**

INGREDIENTS

2 TABLESPOONS EXTRA-VIRGIN OLIVE OIL, PLUS MORE FOR GARNISH

1 MEDIUM YELLOW ONION, BRUNOISED

7 GARLIC CLOVES, MINCED

2 OZ. GUERO OR MANZANA CHILI PEPPERS, STEMMED AND SEEDED

8 OZ. SQUASH, PEELED AND SEEDED

1 LB. SQUASH BLOSSOMS, RINSED WELL, STAMENS REMOVED

SALT, TO TASTE

3 SPRIGS FRESH EPAZOTE

8 CUPS VEGETABLE STOCK

1 CUP SHREDDED QUESO FRESCO, FOR SERVING

LIME WEDGES, FOR GARNISH

DIRECTIONS

1. Place the olive oil in a saucepan and warm it over medium heat. Add the onion, garlic, and chilies and cook until the onion is translucent, about 3 minutes, stirring frequently.

2. Add the squash and half of the squash blossoms and cook for 1 to 2 minutes, stirring frequently. Season the mixture with salt, add the epazote and stock, and simmer the soup until the squash is tender, about 20 minutes.

3. Transfer the soup to a blender and puree until smooth, about 1 minute. Return the soup to the saucepan and stir in the remaining squash blossoms.

4. Ladle the soup into warm bowls, drizzle some olive oil over each portion, top with queso fresco, and garnish with lime wedges.

SOPA DE PAPA

YIELD: **4 SERVINGS**

ACTIVE TIME: **10 MINUTES**

TOTAL TIME: **35 MINUTES**

INGREDIENTS

4 LARGE TOMATOES

2 GARLIC CLOVES

¼ WHITE ONION

1 TABLESPOON EXTRA-VIRGIN
   OLIVE OIL

1 TEASPOON DRIED MEXICAN
   OREGANO

4 YUKON GOLD POTATOES, PEELED
   AND DICED

SALT, TO TASTE

1 CUP SHREDDED QUESO FRESCO

½ BUNCH OF FRESH CILANTRO

DIRECTIONS

1. Bring water to a boil in a small saucepan. Add the tomatoes, garlic, and onion and cook until softened, about 10 minutes. Drain, place the vegetables in a blender, and puree until smooth.

2. Place the olive oil in a medium saucepan and warm over medium heat. Strain the puree into the pan and add the oregano, potatoes, and 2 cups of water. Bring to a simmer and cook until the potatoes are tender but not falling apart, about 15 minutes.

3. Season the soup with salt, ladle it into warmed bowls, and garnish each portion with queso fresco and sprigs of cilantro.

SPLIT PEA SOUP

YIELD: **10 SERVINGS**

ACTIVE TIME: **30 MINUTES**

TOTAL TIME: **2 HOURS**

INGREDIENTS

2 TABLESPOONS AVOCADO OIL

1 LARGE ONION, CHOPPED

1 GARLIC CLOVE, MINCED

2 MEDIUM CARROTS, DICED

2 CELERY STALKS WITH LEAVES,
   DICED

2 BAY LEAVES

1 TEASPOON THYME

1 TEASPOON SEA SALT

FRESHLY GROUND BLACK PEPPER,
   TO TASTE

1 LB. DRIED SPLIT PEAS

½ TEASPOON LEMON ZEST

1 CUP VEGETABLE STOCK

DIRECTIONS

1. In a large pot, heat the oil over medium heat and then sauté the onions until softened and beginning to brown, about 5 minutes.

2. Add the garlic, carrots, and celery and cook for 3 minutes, then add the bay leaves and thyme and season with sea salt and pepper.

3. Add the split peas, lemon zest, and vegetable stock to the pot, stir, bring to a boil, and then simmer, uncovered, for 1½ hours.

4. Remove soup and let cool for about 15 minutes.

5. Using an immersion blender, purée the soup until mostly smooth and silky.

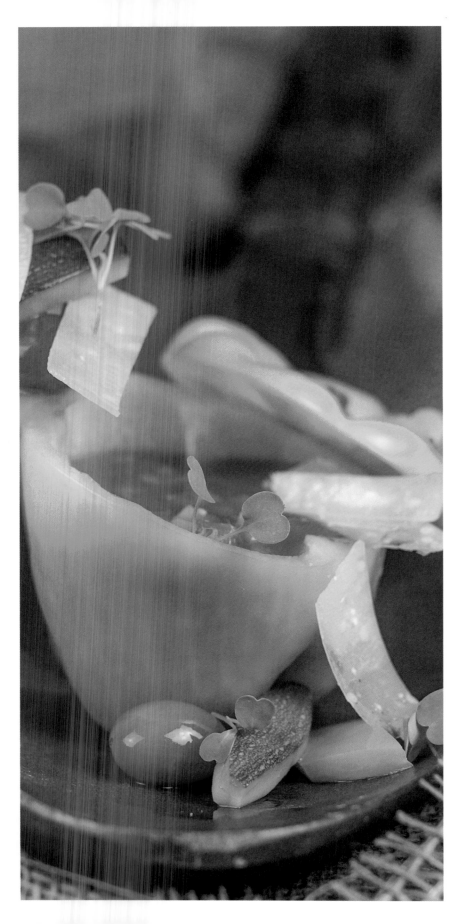

INGREDIENTS

2 TABLESPOONS EXTRA-VIRGIN OLIVE OIL

1 GARLIC CLOVE, MINCED

2 ONIONS, FINELY CHOPPED

1 CARROT, PEELED AND FINELY CHOPPED

½ LEEK, WHITE PART ONLY, FINELY CHOPPED

1 YELLOW BELL PEPPER, SEEDS REMOVED AND FINELY CHOPPED

1 RED BELL PEPPER, SEEDS REMOVED AND FINELY CHOPPED

1 ZUCCHINI, SEEDS REMOVED, FINELY CHOPPED

6 CUPS TOMATO JUICE

½ TEASPOON CHOPPED THYME LEAVES

½ TEASPOON CHOPPED ROSEMARY LEAVES

SALT AND PEPPER, TO TASTE

PARMESAN CHEESE, SHAVED, FOR GARNISH

TO SERVE:

GARLIC CONFIT VEGETABLES

GARLIC CONFIT VEGETABLES

½ CUP EXTRA-VIRGIN OLIVE OIL

1 BULB OF GARLIC, CLOVES REMOVED, PEELED, AND MINCED

8–12 CHERRY TOMATOES

8–12 ZUCCHINI, CHOPPED

8–12 YELLOW BELL PEPPERS, CHOPPED

SALT AND PEPPER, TO TASTE

HEALTHY VEGETABLE MINESTRONE WITH SHAVED PARMESAN

YIELD: **4 TO 6 SERVINGS**

ACTIVE TIME: **45 MINUTES**

TOTAL TIME: **1 HOUR AND 30 MINUTES**

DIRECTIONS

1. In a large saucepan, add the oil and warm over medium heat. Add the garlic, onions, carrot, and leek and cook for 5 minutes, or until soft.

2. Add the bell peppers and cook for 5 minutes. Add the zucchini and cook for 3 minutes.

3. Add the tomato juice, thyme, and rosemary and bring to a boil. Reduce to a simmer and cook for 20 minutes, or until the vegetables are tender.

4. Season with salt and pepper, ladle into bowls, and serve with Garlic Confit Vegetables and garnish with Parmesan.

GARLIC CONFIT VEGETABLES

1. Place the olive oil in a small saucepan and warm.

2. Reduce heat to lowest setting, add the garlic, and cook for 15 minutes, while stirring frequently, until soft and golden.

3. Strain and reserve oil.

4. Return garlic oil to a clean pan and warm.

5. Add the cherry tomatoes, zucchini, and bell peppers, and then remove from heat and let them cool in the oil.

6. Remove with a slotted spoon, season with salt and pepper, and serve.

VEGETABLE QUINOA SOUP

YIELD: **4 SERVINGS**

ACTIVE TIME: **20 MINUTES**

TOTAL TIME: **1 HOUR**

INGREDIENTS

2 TABLESPOONS EXTRA-VIRGIN OLIVE OIL

1 ONION, CHOPPED

2 CARROTS, PEELED AND CHOPPED

2 CELERY STALKS, CHOPPED

½ CUP CORN KERNELS

½ CUP CHOPPED ZUCCHINI

½ CUP CHOPPED RED BELL PEPPER

½ CUP CHOPPED GREEN BELL PEPPER

4 GARLIC CLOVES, MINCED

2 SPRIGS THYME, LEAVES REMOVED AND CHOPPED

2 (14 OZ.) CANS STEWED TOMATOES

1 CUP QUINOA

6 CUPS VEGETABLE STOCK

1 BAY LEAF

PINCH OF RED PEPPER FLAKES

1 (14 OZ.) CAN CHICKPEAS, DRAINED AND RINSED

1½ CUP CUPS FINELY CHOPPED KALE

JUICE OF ½ LEMON

SALT AND PEPPER, TO TASTE

PARMESAN CHEESE, GRATED, FOR GARNISH

DIRECTIONS

1. In a medium saucepan, add the oil and cook over medium heat until warm.

2. Add the onion, carrots, celery, corn, zucchini, and bell peppers and cook for 8 minutes, or until soft.

3. Add the garlic and thyme and cook for 2 minutes. Add the tomatoes, quinoa, stock, bay leaf, and red pepper flakes and bring to a boil. Reduce the heat so that the soup simmers, cover, and cook for 25 minutes.

4. Remove the lid, add the chickpeas and kale, and cook for 5 minutes.

5. Season with the lemon juice, salt, and pepper. Serve in warm bowls and garnish with Parmesan cheese.

VEGETABLE SOUP

INGREDIENTS

2 TABLESPOONS AVOCADO OIL

1 LARGE ONION, ROUGHLY CHOPPED

2 LARGE CARROTS, PEELED AND ROUGHLY CHOPPED

2 LARGE CELERY STALKS WITH LEAVES, ROUGHLY CHOPPED

1 PARSNIP, PEELED AND ROUGHLY CHOPPED

1 LEEK, CLEANED WELL AND ROUGHLY CHOPPED

5 GARLIC CLOVES, SMASHED

9 CUPS VEGETABLE STOCK

2 BAY LEAVES

1 STALK LEMONGRASS, SPLIT INTO FOUR SMALL PIECES

1 HANDFUL CURLY LEAF PARSLEY, ROUGHLY CHOPPED

2 TABLESPOONS SEA SALT

DIRECTIONS

1. In a large stockpot, heat oil and sauté onions for about 5 minutes over medium heat, then add carrots, celery, parsnip, leek, and garlic and sauté for another 5 minutes, until fragrant.

2. Add stock and bay leaves and bring to a boil. Reduce heat and let simmer for about 1 hour, uncovered.

3. After 1 hour, add lemongrass, parsley, and salt and simmer for another 30 minutes.

4. Remove bay leaf and serve.

VEGETABLE SOUP WITH ISRAELI COUSCOUS

YIELD: **4 TO 6 SERVINGS**

ACTIVE TIME: **15 MINUTES**

TOTAL TIME: **45 MINUTES**

INGREDIENTS

2 TABLESPOONS EXTRA-VIRGIN OLIVE OIL

1 ONION, CHOPPED

1 LARGE CARROT, PEELED AND DICED

1 (14 OZ.) CAN DICED TOMATOES

5 GARLIC CLOVES, MINCED

6 CUPS VEGETABLE STOCK

1¼ CUPS ISRAELI COUSCOUS

¼ TEASPOON CUMIN

6 CILANTRO SPRIGS, LEAVES REMOVED AND CHOPPED

SALT AND PEPPER, TO TASTE

⅛ TEASPOON CAYENNE PEPPER

DIRECTIONS

1. In a large saucepan, add the oil and warm over medium heat. Add the onion and carrot and cook for 5 minutes, or until softened.

2. Add the tomatoes, garlic, stock, Israeli couscous, cumin, cilantro, salt, pepper, and cayenne pepper.

3. Bring to a boil, reduce to a simmer, and cook for 8 minutes, or until the couscous is tender.

4. Ladle into warm bowls and serve.

VEGETARIAN RAMEN

YIELD: **4 SERVINGS**

ACTIVE TIME: **15 MINUTES**

TOTAL TIME: **45 MINUTES**

DIRECTIONS

VEGETARIAN DASHI STOCK

1. In a heavy saucepan, add the water and the kombu. Soak for 20 minutes.

2. Remove the kombu and score the surface gently with a knife.

3. Return the kombu to the water and bring to a boil. Remove the kombu immediately, so that the broth doesn't become bitter.

4. Add the dried shiitakes and return to a boil. Turn off heat and let stand until cool.

5. Pass the stock through a fine sieve and refrigerate until ready to use.

RAMEN

1. In a medium saucepan, add the sesame oil and cook over medium heat until warm.

2. Add the garlic and ginger and cook for 3 minutes, or until fragrant.

3. Add the scallions, chili bean paste, and miso, and cook for 1 minute. Add the sake and cook until half of it has evaporated.

4. Add the sesame seed paste, stock, and soy milk, and bring to a boil.

5. Season with salt and pepper, and remove pan from heat.

6. Cook the noodles per manufacturer's instructions. Place the noodles into warm bowls and pour the broth over them. Garnish with scallion greens, toasted sesame seeds, and bean sprouts.

POACHED EGGS

1. Crack each egg into a small, individual bowl.

2. In a medium saucepan, add 3 cups water and 2 tablespoons white vinegar and bring to a boil.

3. Reduce the heat so that the water simmers and gently add the eggs to the water one at a time.

4. Cook for 3 minutes, gently basting the eggs with the poaching water as they cook.

5. Gently remove the eggs with a slotted spoon and place on a paper towel to dry.

6. Season each egg with salt and pepper and serve immediately.

INGREDIENTS

VEGETARIAN DASHI STOCK

3 CUPS WATER

1 OZ. KOMBU

4 DRIED SHIITAKE MUSHROOMS

RAMEN

2 TABLESPOONS SESAME OIL

4 GARLIC CLOVES, MINCED

2-INCH PIECE OF GINGER, MINCED

4 SCALLIONS, SLICED, GREENS
   RESERVED FOR GARNISH

2 TABLESPOONS CHILI BEAN PASTE

2 TABLESPOONS MISO

¼ CUP SAKE

4 TABLESPOONS BLACK-AND-WHITE
   SESAME SEEDS, TOASTED AND
   GROUND INTO A PASTE, PLUS
   MORE FOR GARNISH

2 CUPS VEGETARIAN DASHI STOCK

3 CUPS UNSWEETENED SOY MILK

NOODLES FROM 2 PACKAGES OF
   RAMEN

SALT AND PEPPER, TO TASTE

BEAN SPROUTS, FOR GARNISH

VEGETARIAN YEMENITE SOUP

YIELD: **12 SERVINGS**

ACTIVE TIME: **20 MINUTES**

TOTAL TIME: **1 HOUR AND 15 MINUTES**

INGREDIENTS

3 CUPS CUBED CELERIAC, DIVIDED

2 CUPS SLICED CARROTS, DIVIDED

1 CUP CHOPPED ONION, DIVIDED

3 GARLIC CLOVES

2 TABLESPOONS EXTRA-VIRGIN OLIVE OIL

4 TABLESPOONS TOMATO PASTE

2 TEASPOONS SEA SALT

2 TEASPOONS TURMERIC

1 TEASPOON CUMIN

1 TEASPOON CORIANDER

½ TEASPOON FRESHLY GROUND BLACK PEPPER

8 CUPS VEGETABLE STOCK

1½ CUPS CUBED BUTTERNUT SQUASH

1 CUP CUBED RED BLISS POTATOES

10 OZ. ENOKI MUSHROOMS

DIRECTIONS

1. Combine half the celeriac, carrots, onions, and the garlic in a food processor and pulse until chopped very small.

2. Add the olive oil to a large pot over medium-high heat and add the pureed vegetables and cook for 10 minutes, stirring frequently.

3. Add tomato paste, sea salt, turmeric, cumin, coriander, and pepper and continue cooking for 4 minutes, stirring frequently.

4. Add stock, bring to a boil, and add the remaining celeriac, carrots, and onions, along with the butternut squash and potatoes. Reduce heat and simmer, covered, for 40 minutes.

5. Remove from heat, add the mushrooms, and let stand, covered, for 10 minutes before serving.

VEGAN CAULIFLOWER BLACK BEAN CHILI

YIELD: **4 TO 6 SERVINGS**

ACTIVE TIME: **15 MINUTES**

TOTAL TIME: **45 MINUTES**

INGREDIENTS

2 TABLESPOONS EXTRA-VIRGIN OLIVE OIL

2 RED ONIONS, FINELY CHOPPED

1 RED BELL PEPPER, FINELY CHOPPED

1 YELLOW BELL PEPPER, FINELY CHOPPED

2 GARLIC CLOVES, MINCED

2 HEADS CAULIFLOWER, FLORETS REMOVED AND FINELY CHOPPED

4 (14 OZ.) CANS STEWED TOMATOES

2 CUPS VEGETABLE STOCK

1 TABLESPOON CHILI POWDER, OR TO TASTE

2 (14 OZ.) CANS BLACK BEANS, RINSED AND DRAINED

SALT AND PEPPER, TO TASTE

PARSLEY, CHOPPED, FOR GARNISH

DIRECTIONS

1. In a large saucepan, add the olive oil and cook over medium heat until warm.

2. Add the onions, bell peppers, and garlic. Cook for 7 minutes, or until soft.

3. Add the cauliflower and cook for 5 minutes, or until the florets are lightly browned.

4. Add the tomatoes, stock, and chili powder and bring to a boil. Reduce heat so that the soup simmers, cover, and cook for 15 minutes.

5. Remove the cover and cook for an additional 15 minutes, or until the chili starts to thicken and the cauliflower is tender.

6. Add the beans, cook for another 3 minutes, and season with salt and pepper. Serve in warm bowls and garnish with a sprinkle of parsley.

VEGAN CURRIED LAKSA SOUP

YIELD: **4 TO 6 SERVINGS**

ACTIVE TIME: **20 MINUTES**

TOTAL TIME: **45 MINUTES**

INGREDIENTS

1 TABLESPOON VEGETABLE OIL

LAKSA CURRY PASTE

2 CUPS SLICED SHIITAKE MUSHROOMS

1 CUP SLICED CARROTS

¼ CUP CHOPPED RED BELL PEPPERS

¼ CUP CHOPPED GREEN BELL PEPPERS

¼ CUP CHOPPED GREEN ZUCCHINI

¼ CUP CHOPPED YELLOW SQUASH

4 CUPS VEGETABLE STOCK

1 (14 OZ.) CAN COCONUT MILK

8 OZ. RICE NOODLES

1 CUP CHOPPED KALE

8 OZ. TOFU, CUT INTO ½-INCH CUBES

1 TABLESPOON SOY SAUCE

1 TABLESPOON LIME JUICE

1 TEASPOON SUGAR

SALT AND PEPPER, TO TASTE

THAI CHILES, SEEDS REMOVED, SLICED, FOR GARNISH

CILANTRO, CHOPPED, FOR GARNISH

LAKSA CURRY PASTE

2 TEASPOONS CORIANDER SEEDS

½ TEASPOON FENNEL SEEDS

1 TEASPOON TURMERIC

1-INCH PIECE OF GINGER, PEELED AND MINCED

1 GREEN CHILI, SEEDED AND CHOPPED

½ TEASPOON CAYENNE PEPPER

1 STALK LEMONGRASS

2 GARLIC CLOVES

2 TABLESPOONS CASHEWS, SOAKED IN WARM WATER FOR 10 MINUTES

½ CUP CHOPPED CILANTRO LEAVES

1 TEASPOON LIME JUICE

2 TABLESPOONS WATER

SALT AND PEPPER, TO TASTE

DIRECTIONS

1. In a medium saucepan, add the oil and cook over medium heat until warm. Add the Laksa Curry Paste and cook for 3 minutes, while stirring constantly.

2. Add the mushrooms and cook for 2 minutes.

3. Add the carrots, bell peppers, zucchini, and summer squash and cook for 5 minutes, or until soft.

4. Add the stock and coconut milk and bring to a boil. Reduce heat so that the soup simmers, add the noodles, and cook for 10 minutes.

5. Fold in the kale and tofu, simmer for 2 minutes, and then season with soy sauce, lime juice, sugar, salt, and pepper.

6. Serve in warmed bowls with the Thai chiles and cilantro.

LAKSA CURRY PASTE

1. In a small nonstick pan, add the coriander and fennel seeds and cook for 2 minutes over medium heat, or until they become fragrant.

2. Combine the toasted seeds and remaining ingredients in a food processor and puree until smooth.

VEGAN TOM YAM GUNG WITH TOFU

YIELD: **4 SERVINGS**

ACTIVE TIME: **20 MINUTES**

TOTAL TIME: **45 MINUTES**

INGREDIENTS

4 TABLESPOONS VEGETABLE OIL

1 ONION, FINELY CHOPPED

1 GARLIC CLOVE, MINCED

6 CUPS VEGETABLE STOCK

JUICE OF 2 LIMES

3 KAFFIR LIME LEAVES

3 THAI CHILES, SEEDS REMOVED, SLICED

6 CILANTRO STALKS, LEAVES REMOVED, CHOPPED, AND RESERVED FOR GARNISH

1 LEMONGRASS STALK, BRUISED WITH THE BACK OF A KNIFE

1 TABLESPOON SUGAR

12 OZ. TOFU, CUT INTO ½-INCH CUBES

8 SHIITAKE MUSHROOMS, SLICED

SALT AND PEPPER, TO TASTE

WATERCRESS, FOR GARNISH

BEAN SPROUTS, FOR GARNISH

DIRECTIONS

1. In a medium saucepan, add 2 tablespoons of the oil and cook over medium heat until warm.

2. Add the onion and garlic and cook for 5 minutes, or until soft.

3. Add the stock, lime juice, lime leaves, chiles, cilantro stalks, lemongrass, and sugar and bring to a boil.

4. Reduce the heat so that the soup simmers and cook for 20 minutes.

5. Meanwhile, in a large sauté pan, add the remaining oil and cook over medium heat until warm. Add the tofu and cook for 4 minutes, or until it is lightly browned on all sides. Remove tofu from pan and set aside.

6. Strain the broth through a fine sieve and then return to a clean pan. Add the shiitake mushrooms and bring to a simmer. Add the tofu and cook for 4 additional minutes.

7. Season with salt and pepper, serve in warm bowls, and garnish with watercress, bean sprouts, and cilantro.

YIELD: **4 SERVINGS**

ACTIVE TIME: **25 MINUTES**

TOTAL TIME: **1 HOUR AND 15 MINUTES**

INGREDIENTS

2 TABLESPOONS VEGETABLE OIL

1 ONION, CHOPPED

1 POTATO, PEELED AND CHOPPED

5 PACKED CUPS WATERCRESS, LEAVES REMOVED, STEMS FINELY CHOPPED

2 CUPS VEGETABLE STOCK

1½ CUPS BUTTERMILK

SALT AND PEPPER, TO TASTE

TO SERVE:

POPPY SEED YOGURT

CRISPY POTATO STRIPS

POPPY SEED YOGURT

½ CUP WHOLE MILK YOGURT

1 TABLESPOON POPPY SEEDS

SALT AND PEPPER, TO TASTE

CRISPY POTATO STRIPS

1 YUKON GOLD POTATO, PEELED AND CUT INTO THIN STRIPS

2 CUPS VEGETABLE OIL

SALT AND PEPPER, TO TASTE

WATERCRESS & BUTTERMILK SOUP WITH POPPY SEED YOGURT

DIRECTIONS

1. Place the oil in a medium saucepan and warm over medium heat. Add the onion and cook for 5 minutes, or until soft.

2. Add the potato and cook for 8 minutes.

3. Add the watercress stems and stock and bring to a boil. Reduce to a simmer and cook for 10 minutes, or until the potato is tender.

4. Reserve some watercress leaves for garnish, place the rest in the pan, and simmer for 2 minutes.

5. Transfer to a food processor, blend until smooth, and strain through a fine sieve.

6. Place in a clean pan and add buttermilk. Reheat gently, season with salt and pepper, ladle into warm bowls, and garnish with reserved watercress, Poppy Seed Yogurt, and Crispy Potato Strips.

POPPY SEED YOGURT

1. Place the yogurt and the poppy seeds in a bowl and whisk together.

2. Season with salt and pepper, and place in refrigerator until ready to use.

CRISPY POTATO STRIPS

1. In a small saucepan, add the potato and 3 cups of cold water. Cook over high heat and bring to a boil. Remove the potato strips, submerge in ice water, and set to dry on paper towels.

2. Place the oil in a Dutch oven and heat to 375°F.

3. Place the potato strips in the oil and fry until golden brown.

4. Use a slotted spoon to remove the potato strips, set on a paper towel to drain, and season with salt and pepper.

VEGETARIAN WHITE BEAN SOUP WITH PAN-SEARED RICE CAKE

YIELD: **4 SERVINGS**

ACTIVE TIME: **30 MINUTES**

TOTAL TIME: **1 HOUR AND 30 MINUTES**

INGREDIENTS

2 TABLESPOONS BUTTER

1 ONION, CHOPPED

1 GARLIC CLOVE, MINCED

1 CARROT, PEELED AND CHOPPED

1 CELERY STALK, CHOPPED

½ CUP DRIED WHITE BEANS,
SOAKED OVERNIGHT

2½ CUPS VEGETABLE STOCK

2 (14 OZ.) CANS TOMATOES, FINELY
CHOPPED, JUICE RESERVED

½ TEASPOON CHOPPED ROSEMARY
LEAVES

½ TEASPOON CHOPPED THYME
LEAVES

1 BAY LEAF

SALT AND PEPPER, TO TASTE

OREGANO, CHOPPED, FOR GARNISH

TO SERVE:

PAN-SEARED RICE CAKE

PAN-SEARED RICE CAKE

½ CUP ARBORIO RICE

1 CUP WATER

1 TEASPOON OREGANO, CHOPPED

¼ TEASPOON TABASCO

SALT, TO TASTE

4 TABLESPOONS UNSALTED BUTTER.

DIRECTIONS

1. In a medium saucepan, add the butter and cook over medium heat until melted. Add the onion, garlic, carrot, and celery and cook for 5 minutes, or until the vegetables are soft.

2. Drain the beans and add to the saucepan. Add the stock, tomatoes, rosemary, thyme, and bay leaf. Bring to a boil, reduce heat so that the soup simmers, and cook for approximately 1 hour, or until the beans are tender.

3. Season with salt and pepper and ladle into warm bowls. Garnish with oregano and serve with Pan-Seared Rice Cake.

PAN-SEARED RICE CAKE

1. In a small saucepan, add the rice and water and bring to a boil. Cover, reduce heat to low, and simmer for 10 minutes. Remove lid and stir frequently.

2. Add the oregano, Tabasco, and salt.

3. Lay down a sheet of plastic wrap on a cutting board. Spoon the rice onto the plastic and then roll into a 12-inch log. Cut this into 6-inch logs, transfer to the refrigerator, and chill for an hour.

4. Remove from the refrigerator and cut the logs into 8 slices. In a nonstick pan, add the butter and cook over medium heat until melted. Add the rice cakes and cook for 2 to 3 minutes on each side, or until golden brown.

CHAPTER 5

STEWS & CHILIS

Where do soups end and stews and chilis begin? There's no time to debate that here. But be assured, these recipes are delicious and filling.

BEEF & LAMB STEW

YIELD: **4 SERVINGS**

ACTIVE TIME: **30 MINUTES**

TOTAL TIME: **14 HOURS AND 30 MINUTES**

DIRECTIONS

1. Preheat the oven to 250°F.

2. Drain the chickpeas. Place the oil in a Dutch oven and cook over medium heat until warm.

3. Add the onion, garlic, parsnips, carrots, cumin, turmeric, and ginger and cook for 2 minutes.

4. Add the brisket and lamb and cook for 5 minutes, or until all sides are browned.

5. Add the stock and bring to a simmer.

6. Add the chickpeas, potato, zucchini, tomatoes, lentils, bay leaf, and cilantro.

7. Cover, place in the oven, and cook for 1 hour and 15 minutes, or until the meat is tender.

8. Begin cooking the Long-Grain Rice 30 minutes before serving.

9. Once the stew is ready, remove the lid and skim the fat from the top of the soup. Season with salt and pepper and ladle into warmed bowls with the rice. Garnish with lemon wedges and chilies.

LONG-GRAIN RICE

1. In a medium saucepan, bring the water and salt to a boil.

2. Add the rice, reduce heat to low, cover, and cook for 15 minutes while stirring occasionally.

3. Turn off flame, and let stand for 5 minutes before serving.

INGREDIENTS

½ CUP CHICKPEAS, SOAKED OVERNIGHT

1½ TABLESPOONS EXTRA-VIRGIN OLIVE OIL

1 SMALL ONION, PEELED AND CHOPPED

5 GARLIC CLOVES, MINCED

¾ CUP SLICED PARSNIPS

¾ CUP SLICED CARROTS

1 TEASPOON CUMIN

¼ TEASPOON TURMERIC

1½ TABLESPOONS PEELED AND MINCED GINGER

5 OZ. BRISKET, CLEANED AND CUT INTO ¼-INCH CUBES

5 OZ. LAMB SHOULDER, CLEANED AND CUT INTO ¼-INCH CUBES

4 CUPS BEEF OR VEAL STOCK

1 SMALL POTATO, PEELED AND CUT INTO CHUNKS

1 SMALL ZUCCHINI, SLICED

8 OZ. FRESH TOMATO, DICED

2 TABLESPOONS BROWN LENTILS

1 BAY LEAF

½ BUNCH OF FRESH CILANTRO, CHOPPED

SALT AND PEPPER, TO TASTE

LEMON WEDGES, FOR GARNISH

FRESH CHILIES, CHOPPED, FOR GARNISH

TO SERVE:

LONG-GRAIN RICE

LONG-GRAIN RICE

2 CUPS WATER

1 TEASPOON SALT

1 CUP LONG-GRAIN RICE

YIELD: **4 SERVINGS**

ACTIVE TIME: **45 MINUTES**

TOTAL TIME: **3 HOURS**

INGREDIENTS

4 CHICKEN LEGS (THIGH AND DRUMSTICK)

SEA SALT, TO TASTE

4 TABLESPOONS EXTRA-VIRGIN OLIVE OIL, DIVIDED

1 LARGE ONION, THINLY SLICED

6 GARLIC CLOVES, HALVED

2 TABLESPOONS HONEY

1 TABLESPOON TOMATO PASTE

¾ TEASPOON TURMERIC

½ TEASPOON CINNAMON

1 (14.5 OZ.) CAN OF WHOLE PEELED TOMATOES

3 CUPS CHICKEN STOCK

1 LEMON

1½ TEASPOONS SUGAR

1 TABLESPOON TOASTED SESAME SEEDS, FOR GARNISH

½ CUP TORN MINT, FOR GARNISH

CHICKEN & TOMATO STEW WITH CARAMELIZED LEMON

DIRECTIONS

1. Pat chicken dry and season with salt. Let sit at room temperature for at least 15 minutes and up to 1 hour ahead, or cover and refrigerate for up to 24 hours.

2. Add 2 tablespoons oil in a large Dutch oven over medium-high heat and cook chicken until deep golden brown on both sides, about 6 minutes per side; adjust heat as necessary to avoid burning. Transfer chicken to a plate, leaving drippings behind.

3. Add onion to pot and cook, stirring often, until softened, 6 to 8 minutes. Add garlic and cook, stirring often until onion begins to brown around the edges, about 3 minutes. Stir in honey, tomato paste, turmeric, and cinnamon and cook until fragrant, about 2 minutes. Add tomatoes and juices and smash tomatoes with a wooden spoon until pieces are no larger than 1 inch.

4. Return chicken to pot, pour in stock (it should barely cover chicken), and bring to a simmer. Reduce heat to low, mostly cover pot with lid, and gently simmer until chicken is tender and juices thicken, 1 hour and 10 minutes to 1 hour and 20 minutes.

5. Meanwhile, trim the top and bottom from the lemon and cut lengthwise into quarters; remove seeds and white pith in the center. Thinly slice quarters crosswise into quarter-moons.

6. Place the lemon pieces in a medium skillet, cover with water, and bring to a boil. Cook for 3 minutes, then drain and pat dry with paper towels. Transfer to a small bowl, sprinkle with sugar, and toss to coat.

7. Wipe out the skillet and heat 2 tablespoons oil over medium-high. Arrange lemon pieces in a single layer in the skillet. Cook, turning halfway through, until deeply browned in most spots, about 3 minutes. Transfer back to the bowl and season with salt.

8. Ladle stew into bowls and garnish with caramelized lemon, sesame seeds, and mint.

CHILI CON CARNE

YIELD: **4 TO 6 SERVINGS**

ACTIVE TIME: **20 MINUTES**

TOTAL TIME: **2 HOURS**

INGREDIENTS

¼ CUP VEGETABLE OIL

1 GREEN BELL PEPPER, CHOPPED

1 ONION, PEELED AND CHOPPED

2 LBS. GROUND BEEF

2 BEEF BOUILLON CUBES, CRUSHED

1 CUP RED WINE

2 (14 OZ.) CANS STEWED
    TOMATOES, CHOPPED

2 GARLIC CLOVES, MINCED

6 TABLESPOONS TOMATO PASTE

1 TEASPOON PAPRIKA

2 TEASPOONS CHILI POWDER

1 TEASPOON CAYENNE POWDER

2 TEASPOONS CHOPPED BASIL
    LEAVES

1 TEASPOON CHOPPED OREGANO
    LEAVES

2 TABLESPOONS CHOPPED PARSLEY
    LEAVES

½ TEASPOON TABASCO

1 (14 OZ.) CAN KIDNEY BEANS

3 TABLESPOONS ALL-PURPOSE
    FLOUR

2 TABLESPOONS CORNMEAL

½ CUP WATER

SALT AND PEPPER, TO TASTE

GRATED MOZZARELLA CHEESE, FOR
    GARNISH

DIRECTIONS

1. In a large saucepan, add the oil and cook over medium heat until warm.

2. Add the bell pepper and onion, and cook for 5 minutes, or until soft.

3. Add the ground beef and cook for 10 minutes, or until nicely browned.

4. Add the bouillon cubes and red wine, and cook for 2 minutes.

5. Add the stewed tomatoes, garlic, tomato paste, paprika, chili powder, cayenne pepper, basil, oregano, parsley, and Tabasco and bring to a boil.

6. Reduce heat to the lowest setting, cover, and cook for 1 hour, stirring occasionally.

7. Add the kidney beans and cook for an additional 15 minutes.

8. In a mixing bowl, combine the flour, cornmeal, and water. Add this mixture to the chili and cook for an additional 10 minutes. The chili should be nice and thick at this point.

9. Set the oven to the broiler setting.

10. Once chili is cooked, sprinkle a healthy amount of mozzarella on top and place the saucepan under the broiler until the cheese is melted. Serve in warmed bowls with tortilla chips.

INGREDIENTS

1 JALAPEÑO

1 TABLESPOON EXTRA-VIRGIN OLIVE OIL

1 LB. PORK STEW MEAT, CUT INTO ½-INCH PIECES

1 ONION, CHOPPED

2 GARLIC CLOVES, MINCED

1 (14 OZ.) CAN DICED STEWED TOMATOES

2 TOMATILLOS, HUSKED AND CHOPPED

4 CUPS CHICKEN STOCK

1 TEASPOON CHOPPED OREGANO LEAVES

PINCH OF GROUND CLOVES

TO SERVE:

LONG-GRAIN RICE

LONG-GRAIN RICE

1 CUP LONG-GRAIN RICE

2 CUPS WATER

1 TEASPOON SALT

YIELD: **4 SERVINGS**

ACTIVE TIME: **20 MINUTES**

TOTAL TIME: **1 HOUR AND 15 MINUTES**

CHILI VERDE

DIRECTIONS

1. Over an open flame, char the jalapeño. Place in a bowl, cover, and let stand for 5 minutes.

2. Cut jalapeño into 8 slices and reserve for garnish. Remove seeds and finely chop the remaining pepper.

3. In a medium saucepan, add the olive oil and cook over medium-high heat until warm.

4. Add the pork and cook for 5 minutes.

5. Add the onions and garlic and cook for 5 minutes, or until the pork is nicely browned.

6. Add the tomatoes, tomatillos, stock, oregano, and cloves.

7. Bring to a boil, reduce the heat to low, cover, and cook for 20 minutes, while stirring occasionally.

8. Remove 2 cups of the broth, taking care not to remove any of the pork, and place it in a food processor. Puree until smooth.

9. Return the puree to the saucepan and cook for 25 minutes, while stirring occasionally, until the pork is tender.

10. Ladle into warm bowls, serve with long-grain rice, and garnish with reserved jalapeño.

LONG-GRAIN RICE

1. In a medium saucepan, bring the water and salt to a boil.

2. Add the rice, reduce heat to low, cover, and cook for 15 minutes while stirring occasionally.

3. Turn off heat, and let stand for 5 minutes before serving.

CINCINNATI CHILI

YIELD: **4 TO 6 SERVINGS**

ACTIVE TIME: **15 MINUTES**

TOTAL TIME: **1 HOUR AND 30 MINUTES**

INGREDIENTS

2 TABLESPOONS VEGETABLE OIL

1 ONION, PEELED AND CHOPPED

1½ LBS. GROUND BEEF

2 TABLESPOONS CHILI POWDER, OR TO TASTE

1 TEASPOON CINNAMON

1 TEASPOON CUMIN

¼ TEASPOON ALLSPICE

¼ TEASPOON GROUND CLOVES

2 BAY LEAVES

2 CUPS BEEF STOCK

1 CUP TOMATO SAUCE

2 TABLESPOONS APPLE CIDER VINEGAR

¼ TEASPOON CAYENNE PEPPER

1 OZ. UNSWEETENED CHOCOLATE

SALT AND PEPPER, TO TASTE

GRATED CHEDDAR CHEESE, FOR GARNISH

PARSLEY, CHOPPED, FOR GARNISH

TO SERVE:

SPAGHETTI, COOKED ACCORDING TO MANUFACTURER'S INSTRUCTIONS

DIRECTIONS

1. In a medium saucepan, add the vegetable oil and cook over medium heat until warm.

2. Add the onion and cook for 5 minutes, or until soft.

3. Add the beef and use a wooden spoon to break it up as it cooks. Cook for 5 minutes, or until evenly browned.

4. Add the chili powder, cinnamon, cumin, allspice, cloves, bay leaves, beef stock, tomato sauce, vinegar, and cayenne pepper and bring to a boil.

5. Reduce heat to low, cover, and cook for 1 hour, stirring occasionally.

6. Right before serving, remove from heat, add the chocolate, and season with salt and pepper.

7. Place a bed of spaghetti in a bowl. Pour chili on top, garnish with cheddar cheese, additional spaghetti, and parsley and serve.

YIELD: **6 SERVINGS**

ACTIVE TIME: **30 MINUTES**

TOTAL TIME: **3 HOURS**

INGREDIENTS

2¼ LBS. BONELESS SHORT RIBS

1 TEASPOON SEA SALT, PLUS MORE TO TASTE

½ TEASPOON BLACK PEPPER, PLUS MORE TO TASTE

¼ CUP PLUS 5 TABLESPOONS AVOCADO OIL

3 GARLIC CLOVES, PEELED AND SMASHED

4 TABLESPOONS TOMATO PASTE

¾ LB. VINE-RIPE TOMATOES, QUARTERED

1½ CUPS WATER

JUICE OF 1 MEDIUM LEMON, PLUS MORE TO TASTE

1 TEASPOON SWEET PAPRIKA

3 BAY LEAVES, DIVIDED

1 SMALL JALAPEŃO, SLICED INTO ⅛-INCH ROUNDS

1 TEASPOON SUGAR

1 LB. OKRA, STEMS TRIMMED

1 BUNCH MINT

1 CUP BASMATI RICE

1 TEASPOON CORIANDER SEEDS

1½ CUPS BOILING WATER

EGYPTIAN SHORT RIB & OKRA STEW

DIRECTIONS

1. Preheat the oven to 350°F.

2. Slice meat into 2-inch cubes and season all sides with salt and pepper.

3. Add ¼ cup oil to a large heavy-bottom pot over medium-high heat. Brown meat on all sides, about 5 minutes, adding garlic as meat is nearly browned.

4. Remove meat from the pot and add tomato paste. Cook for 30 seconds, stirring constantly. Add tomatoes in small batches, squeezing and juicing them into the pan before adding.

5. Add the water, lemon juice, paprika, 1 bay leaf, and 3 to 5 slices of jalapeño. Add meat back to pot, spacing evenly, and sprinkle it with the sugar. Turn down heat to low and simmer uncovered while preparing the okra.

6. Add 3 tablespoons of oil to pan over high heat. Once the oil is hot, add the okra, tossing until bright green and lightly blistered, 1 to 2 minutes. Remove from heat, toss with ¼ teaspoon salt and a squeeze of lemon juice.

7. Add okra to the pot, spacing evenly around the meat. Add 6 to 10 mint leaves, cover, and bake for 2 hours, checking every 30 minutes. If liquid reduces too much add water.

8. After 2 hours, the meat should be fork tender. Turn on the broiler and broil, uncovered, for 10 to 12 minutes, until dark and caramelized.

9. Meanwhile, add 2 tablespoons oil to a small saucepan over high heat. Add the rice and toast, stirring until the grains are too hot to touch. Add 2 bay leaves, coriander, and boiling water, bring to a boil, then lower heat and simmer, covered, for 20 minutes.

10. Remove rice from heat and let stand for 10 minutes. Gently fluff rice with a spoon, then cover until ready to serve.

11. Remove stew from the oven. Season to taste and sprinkle with a handful of mint leaves. Serve warm with rice.

ITALIAN LAMB STEW

YIELD: **4 TO 6 SERVINGS**

ACTIVE TIME: **30 MINUTES**

TOTAL TIME: **1 HOUR AND 30 MINUTES**

INGREDIENTS

2 TABLESPOONS EXTRA-VIRGIN
OLIVE OIL

2 LBS. LEG OF LAMB, CUT INTO
1-INCH PIECES

4 GARLIC CLOVES, MINCED

¾ CUP RED WINE

2 CUPS CHICKEN STOCK

3 (14 OZ.) CANS STEWED
TOMATOES, CHOPPED

2 TEASPOONS DRIED OREGANO

2 BAY LEAVES

6 POTATOES, PEELED AND CUT
INTO ½-INCH PIECES

2 CUPS CHOPPED GREEN BEANS

2 RED BELL PEPPERS, SEEDS
REMOVED AND CUT INTO 1-INCH
PIECES

2 ZUCCHINI, HALVED AND SLICED

¼ CUP CHOPPED PARSLEY LEAVES

SALT AND PEPPER, TO TASTE

DIRECTIONS

1. In a large saucepan, add the oil and cook over medium-high heat until warm.

2. Add the lamb and cook for 5 minutes, or until evenly browned.

3. Add the garlic and cook for 2 minutes.

4. Add the wine and cook until it is reduced by half.

5. Add the stock, tomatoes, oregano, and bay leaves and reduce the heat so that the soup simmers. Cook for 45 minutes, or until the lamb is tender.

6. Raise the heat to medium-high and add the potatoes, green beans, bell peppers, and zucchini. Cook for 15 minutes, or until the vegetables are tender.

7. Remove the bay leaves, add the parsley, and season with salt and pepper. Serve in warmed bowls with crusty bread.

LAMB & OKRA STEW

YIELD: **4 SERVINGS**

ACTIVE TIME: **15 MINUTES**

TOTAL TIME: **55 MINUTES**

INGREDIENTS

2 TABLESPOONS VEGETABLE OIL

2 ONIONS, PEELED AND CHOPPED

1½ LBS. LAMB SHOULDER, CUT INTO ½-INCH PIECES

2 TABLESPOONS GROUND TURMERIC

½ CUP TOMATO PASTE

4 CUPS LAMB STOCK

2 GARLIC CLOVES

20 FRESH OKRA, CUT IN ¼-INCH SLICES

SALT AND PEPPER, TO TASTE

DIRECTIONS

1. In a medium saucepan, add the oil and cook over medium heat until warm.

2. Add the onions and cook for 5 minutes or until soft.

3. Add the lamb shoulder and turmeric and cook for 5 minutes, or until the lamb is evenly browned.

4. Add the tomato paste, stock, and garlic and bring to a boil. Reduce heat so that the soup simmers and cook for 30 minutes, until the meat is very tender.

5. Add the okra and simmer for 5 more minutes.

6. Season with salt and pepper and serve in warmed bowls.

LAMB STEW WITH CANDIED CARROTS & GARLIC ROASTED LITTLE CREAMER POTATOES

DIRECTIONS

1. Preheat the oven to 250°F.

2. In a mixing bowl, add flour and then the lamb pieces. Toss until each piece is evenly coated.

3. In a Dutch oven, add the butter and cook over medium heat until melted.

4. Add the lamb and any additional flour. Cook for 5 minutes, or until the lamb is nicely browned.

5. Add the onion, carrot, leek, and garlic and cook for 5 minutes, or until soft.

6. Add the wine and cook for 5 minutes.

7. Add the stock, bay leaves, and thyme, raise heat to medium-high, and bring to a boil.

8. Cover Dutch oven and place it in the oven for 1 hour, removing every 15 minutes to stir the contents.

9. While the stew is cooking, warm the oil in a small sauté pan and then add the sausage. Cook for 5 minutes, or until nicely browned

10. Increase the oven temperature to 325°F. Remove cover, add sausage, olives, and sherry vinegar. Cook for an additional 20 minutes, or until lamb is tender.

11. Skim any fat off the top and season with salt and pepper.

12. Remove the thyme and bay leaves and serve in bowls with Candied Carrots and Garlic Roasted Little Creamer Potatoes.

GARLIC ROASTED LITTLE CREAMER POTATOES

1. Preheat the oven to 350°F.

2. Place the potatoes on a baking tray, drizzle with the olive oil, and season with salt and pepper.

3. Place in oven and cook for 10 minutes.

4. Remove the tray from oven and sprinkle the garlic over the potatoes. Return to the oven and cook for an additional 20 minutes, or until the potatoes are cooked through

5. Remove from pan, toss with the chopped parsley, and serve.

CANDIED CARROTS

1. In a medium saucepan, bring 6 cups of water to boil. Add the carrots and cook for 8 minutes, or until tender.

2. Drain the carrots. Reduce the heat to the lowest possible setting and return the carrots to the pan. Stir in butter, brown sugar, salt, and pepper. Cook for 3 to 5 minutes, while stirring, until the carrots are evenly coated.

YIELD: **4 TO 6 SERVINGS**

ACTIVE TIME: **30 MINUTES**

TOTAL TIME: **2 HOURS**

INGREDIENTS

⅓ CUP ALL-PURPOSE FLOUR

2 LBS. BUTTERFLIED LEG OF
LAMB, FAT AND SILVER SKIN
REMOVED, CUT INTO 1-INCH
PIECES

4 TABLESPOONS UNSALTED
BUTTER

1 ONION, PEELED AND
CHOPPED

1 CARROT, PEELED AND
CHOPPED

½ LEEK, WHITE PART ONLY,
CHOPPED

5 GARLIC CLOVES, MINCED

1 CUP RED WINE

2 CUPS LAMB OR BEEF STOCK

2 BAY LEAVES

6 THYME SPRIGS

1 TABLESPOON VEGETABLE OIL

8 OZ. LAMB OR PORK SAUSAGE,
THICKLY SLICED

½ CUP SLICED KALAMATA
OLIVES

1 TABLESPOON SHERRY
VINEGAR

SALT AND PEPPER, TO TASTE

TO SERVE:

GARLIC ROASTED LITTLE
CREAMER POTATOES

CANDIED CARROTS

**GARLIC ROASTED LITTLE
CREAMER POTATOES**

1 LB. BABY CREAMER POTATOES

2 TABLESPOONS EXTRA-VIRGIN
OLIVE OIL

SALT AND PEPPER, TO TASTE

6 CLOVES GARLIC, MINCED

PARSLEY, CHOPPED

CANDIED CARROTS

5 CARROTS, PEELED AND CUT
INTO 1-INCH PIECES

2 TABLESPOONS UNSALTED
BUTTER

¼ CUP LIGHT BROWN SUGAR

SALT AND PEPPER, TO TASTE

INGREDIENTS

1 (1¼ LBS.) LOBSTER

1 LB. PEI MUSSELS, WASHED AND DEBEARDED

12 LITTLE NECK CLAMS, WASHED AND SCRUBBED

2 TABLESPOONS EXTRA-VIRGIN OLIVE OIL

½ LARGE FENNEL BULB, SLICED THIN

2 SHALLOTS, MINCED

3 GARLIC CLOVES, MINCED

1 (6 OZ.) CAN TOMATO PASTE

1 CUP RED WINE (ZINFANDEL PREFERRED)

1 (28 OZ.) CAN WHOLE SAN MARZANO TOMATOES, LIGHTLY CRUSHED BY HAND

1 CUP WHITE WINE (CHARDONNAY PREFERRED)

2 CUPS FISH STOCK

2 BAY LEAVES

1 TEASPOON CRUSHED RED PEPPER FLAKES

SALT AND PEPPER TO TASTE

1 LB. HALIBUT, SKINNED AND CUT INTO LARGE CUBES

1 LOAF OF SOURDOUGH OR CRUSTY ITALIAN BREAD, TO SERVE

LOBSTER CIOPPINO

DIRECTIONS

1. Place 3 inches of water in a Dutch oven and bring to a boil. Place the lobster in the pot, cover, and cook for 5 to 7 minutes, until the shell is a bright, reddish orange. Remove the lobster from the pot and set aside. Drain the cooking liquid and return the Dutch oven to the stove.

2. Add 2 cups of water and bring to a boil. Add your cleaned mussels and clams, cover the pot, and cook for 3 to 5 minutes, until the majority of the shells have opened. Drain, setting aside the clams and mussels while reserving the liquid. Discard any clams and mussels that do not open.

3. Place the Dutch oven over medium-high heat and add the olive oil. When the oil is warm, add the fennel and cook for 3 minutes until the fennel is soft and slightly translucent.

4. Add the shallots and garlic. Stir and cook for 5 minutes.

5. Add the tomato paste and stir to incorporate. Add the red wine and cook until it is almost evaporated, about 5 minutes. Scrape the bottom with a wooden spoon to remove any bits that are stuck.

6. Add the tomatoes, white wine, fish stock, bay leaves, red pepper flakes, and a pinch of salt and pepper. Reduce the heat to medium-low, cover, and cook for 30 minutes.

7. While the stew is cooking, use a lobster cracker or a heavy knife to crack the lobster open. Remove the tail first. Using a towel, grab the tail where it connects to the body and twist until it detaches. Do this over a bowl to catch any juices that are released. Use the cracker or knife to crack open the shell and remove the meat. If you are using a knife, press the tail flat on a cutting board, top side down. Carefully cut down the length of the tail and remove the meat.

8. If using a cracker, crack each claw at the joint, then crack the top part of the claw until the shell opens. Grab the bottom piece of the claw and twist it sideways. Once loose, pull straight back to remove the shell. The cartilage should also come out with it. Remove all of the meat and discard the shells. If you are using a knife, use the flat of the knife to crack the shells open. Set the lobster meat aside.

9. Remove the legs from the lobster and add the remaining carcass to the pot. Uncover the pot and cook for 20 minutes.

10. Add the halibut to the pot and cook for 5 minutes. Add the lobster meat, clams, mussels, and the reserved cooking liquid and cook for 2 minutes. Serve with a loaf of sourdough or crusty Italian bread.

MEDITERRANEAN LAMB & LENTIL STEW

YIELD: **4 TO 6 SERVINGS**

ACTIVE TIME: **20 MINUTES**

TOTAL TIME: **45 MINUTES**

INGREDIENTS

2 TABLESPOONS EXTRA-VIRGIN OLIVE OIL

2 LBS. LAMB SHOULDER, CUT INTO ½-INCH PIECES

2 ONIONS, PEELED AND CHOPPED

4 CARROTS, PEELED AND CHOPPED

4 GARLIC CLOVES, MINCED

1½ CUPS RED LENTILS

6 CUPS CHICKEN STOCK

2 (14 OZ.) CANS STEWED TOMATOES, DICED

2 TEASPOONS CHOPPED THYME LEAVES

1 TEASPOONS CHOPPED SAGE LEAVES

4 CUPS CHOPPED BABY SPINACH

ZEST AND JUICE OF 2 LEMONS

SALT AND PEPPER, TO TASTE

RICOTTA CHEESE, FOR GARNISH

DIRECTIONS

1. In a medium saucepan, add the olive oil and cook over medium heat until warm.

2. Add the lamb and cook for 5 minutes, or until evenly browned.

3. Add the onions, carrots, and garlic, and cook for 5 minutes, or until soft.

4. Add the lentils, stock, tomatoes, and herbs and bring to a boil. Reduce the heat so that the soup simmers and cook for 20 minutes, or until the lentils are tender.

5. Add the spinach, lemon zest, and lemon juice and season with salt and pepper.

6. Serve in warmed bowls with a sprinkle of ricotta cheese.

MEXICAN BEEF CHILI WITH NACHOS

YIELD: **4 SERVINGS**

ACTIVE TIME: **20 MINUTES**

TOTAL TIME: **1 HOUR AND 15 MINUTES**

INGREDIENTS

3 TABLESPOONS EXTRA-VIRGIN OLIVE OIL

16 OZ. BEEF ROUND ROAST, CUT INTO PIECES

3 ONIONS, PEELED AND CHOPPED

3 GARLIC CLOVES, MINCED

2 RED CHILIES, SEEDED AND FINELY CHOPPED

1 TEASPOON CAYENNE PEPPER

1 TEASPOON GROUND CUMIN

6 CUPS BEEF OR VEAL STOCK

2 BAY LEAVES

3 TABLESPOONS TOMATO PASTE

1 (14 OZ.) CAN CANNELLINI BEANS, DRAINED AND RINSED

1 (14 OZ.) CAN BLACK BEANS, DRAINED AND RINSED

1 BAG TORTILLA CHIPS

8 OZ. MONTEREY JACK CHEESE, GRATED

1 JALAPEÑO, SLICED

SOUR CREAM

CILANTRO, CHOPPED

SALT AND PEPPER, TO TASTE

DIRECTIONS

1. In a large pan, add the oil and the meat and cook over medium-high heat until the meat is golden brown.

2. Reduce the heat. Add the onions, garlic, and chilies and cook for 5 minutes, or until soft.

3. Add the cayenne pepper and cumin, cook for 2 minutes, and then add the stock, bay leaves, and tomato paste.

4. Bring to a boil, reduce heat so that the soup simmers, and cook for 30 to 40 minutes, or until the meat is tender.

5. Meanwhile, preheat the oven to 350°F.

6. Place ⅓ of the cannellini beans and black beans in a bowl and mash them with a fork.

7. Once the meat is tender, add the mashed beans, which will help thicken the soup.

8. On a baking tray, lay out the tortilla chips. Sprinkle with cheese and jalapeño slices, and place in the oven. Cook for 5 minutes, or until cheese is melted. Remove from oven and top with sour cream and cilantro.

9. Add the remaining beans to the soup. Adjust seasoning to taste and then serve in warmed bowls with the nachos.

MOROCCAN BEEF & BEAN STEW WITH HONEY-GLAZED MOROCCAN CARROTS

DIRECTIONS

1. In a large saucepan, bring 6 cups of the water to a boil. Place the marrow bone in the pan and cook for 5 minutes. Remove the marrow bone and discard the water. Run the marrow bone under cold water and then return to the pan.

2. Add the sirloin, onion, kidney beans, and remaining water to the pan. Bring to a boil, then reduce heat and simmer for 1 hour.

3. Add the drained lentils, tomatoes, celery, tomato paste, ginger, and saffron threads. Simmer for an additional 15 minutes, adding water if necessary, or until the lentils start to soften.

4. In a small bowl, add the flour. While whisking continuously, slowly add ½ cup of the broth, taking care not to create any lumps.

5. Add another ½ cup of simmering broth to the flour mixture and then set aside.

6. Add the rice to the broth and cook for 20 minutes, or until rice is cooked.

7. Just before serving, add the flour mixture to the soup, stirring vigorously until well combined.

8. Add the cilantro and parsley and cook for 3 minutes.

9. Remove marrow bone and ladle into warmed bowls. Serve with Honey-Glazed Moroccan Carrots and Charred Lemon Wedges.

HONEY-GLAZED MOROCCAN CARROTS

1. Preheat the oven to 400°F.

2. In a bowl, add the olive oil, honey, cumin, ginger, and cinnamon and stir until combined.

3. Add the carrots and toss to coat.

4. Place the carrots on a baking tray lined with parchment. Season with salt and pepper, place in the oven, and roast for 15 minutes, or until tender and lightly golden brown. Remove from the oven and serve.

CHARRED LEMON WEDGES

1. In a dry, nonstick pan, add the lemons and cook over medium heat on each open side for 3 minutes, or until charred. Remove, let cool, and serve.

YIELD: **4 SERVINGS**

ACTIVE TIME: **45 MINUTES**

TOTAL TIME: **14 HOURS**

INGREDIENTS

12 CUPS WATER

1 MARROW BONE

12 OZ. BEEF SIRLOIN, CUT INTO ½-INCH PIECES

1 LARGE ONION, CHOPPED

¼ CUP DRIED KIDNEY BEANS, SOAKED IN WATER OVERNIGHT

4 TABLESPOONS BROWN LENTILS, RINSED

2 TOMATOES, CHOPPED

1 CELERY STALK, CHOPPED

2 TEASPOONS TOMATO PASTE

⅛ TEASPOON GROUND GINGER

⅛ TEASPOON SAFFRON THREADS

3 TABLESPOONS ALL-PURPOSE FLOUR

4 TABLESPOONS LONG-GRAIN RICE

4 TABLESPOONS CHOPPED CILANTRO

2 TABLESPOONS CHOPPED PARSLEY

SALT AND PEPPER, TO TASTE

TO SERVE:

HONEY-GLAZED MOROCCAN CARROTS

CHARRED LEMON WEDGES

HONEY-GLAZED MOROCCAN CARROTS

1 TABLESPOON EXTRA-VIRGIN OLIVE OIL

2 TEASPOONS HONEY

½ TEASPOON CUMIN

¼ TEASPOON GROUND GINGER

¼ TEASPOON CINNAMON

2 CARROTS, PEELED AND CHOPPED

SALT AND PEPPER, TO TASTE

CHARRED LEMON WEDGES

2 LEMONS, CUT INTO 8 PIECES

INGREDIENTS

2 CUPS MILK

2 CUPS HEAVY CREAM

1 CUP CHOPPED GREEN BELL PEPPER

1 CUP ONION, CHOPPED

1 GARLIC CLOVE, MINCED

25 OYSTERS, RINSED, SHUCKED, AND MEAT REMOVED, LIQUID RESERVED

1½ CUPS QUARTERED SMALL CREAMER OR FINGERLING POTATOES

1 TEASPOON PAPRIKA, PLUS MORE FOR GARNISH

2 TOMATOES, CONCASSE (SEE PAGE 339)

1 TEASPOON LEMON JUICE

1 TABLESPOON CAPERS, CHOPPED

SALT AND PEPPER, TO TASTE

PARSLEY, CHOPPED, FOR GARNISH

TO SERVE:

HERB BUTTER

HERB BUTTER

½ CUP UNSALTED BUTTER, BROUGHT TO ROOM TEMPERATURE

1 TABLESPOON VEGETABLE OIL

1 SMALL SHALLOT, FINELY CHOPPED

1 TEASPOON LEMON JUICE

2 TEASPOONS CHOPPED PARSLEY

1 TEASPOON CHOPPED TARRAGON

1 TEASPOON CHOPPED CHIVES

1 TEASPOON CHOPPED MARJORAM

SALT AND PEPPER, TO TASTE

OYSTER STEW WITH HERB BUTTER

YIELD: **4 TO 6 SERVINGS**

ACTIVE TIME: **45 MINUTES**

TOTAL TIME: **1 HOUR AND 30 MINUTES**

DIRECTIONS

1. Add the milk, cream, bell pepper, onion, garlic, and oyster liquid to a medium saucepan. Cook over low heat for 10 minutes, or until the pepper is tender.

2. Meanwhile, bring water to boil in a saucepan. Add the potatoes and cook for 5 minutes, or until soft. Remove and add to the other saucepan.

3. Add the oysters and cook for 3 to 4 minutes, while stirring occasionally, until the oysters are plump.

4. Add the paprika, tomatoes, lemon juice, and capers. Season to taste with salt and pepper, ladle into bowls, place a small ring of the Herb Butter in the center, and garnish with parsley and paprika.

HERB BUTTER

1. Place the butter in a bowl and whisk until it is nice and creamy.

2. Place the oil in a sauté pan and cook over medium heat until warm. Add the shallot and cook 2 to 3 minutes, or until soft.

3. Add the lemon juice, remove the pan from heat, and set aside to cool.

4. When cool, transfer the contents of the pan to the butter. Add the chopped herbs and mix to combine. Season with salt and pepper and roll into thin logs. Cover with plastic wrap and refrigerate until ready to use.

PORK & APPLE STEW

YIELD: **SERVES 4 TO 6**

ACTIVE TIME: **20 MINUTES**

TOTAL TIME: **1 HOUR AND 15 MINUTES**

INGREDIENTS

1½ LBS. PORK SHOULDER, CUBED

⅓ CUP ALL-PURPOSE FLOUR

2 TABLESPOONS VEGETABLE OIL

2 TABLESPOONS UNSALTED BUTTER

2 ONIONS, DICED

4 GARLIC CLOVES, MINCED

1 TABLESPOON CHOPPED THYME
LEAVES

1 TABLESPOON CHOPPED
ROSEMARY LEAVES

2 POTATOES, PEELED AND CHOPPED
INTO ½-INCH CUBES

1 CUP RED WINE

6 CUPS VEAL STOCK

2 GRANNY SMITH APPLES, PEELED,
CORED, AND CHOPPED

SALT AND PEPPER, TO TASTE

DIRECTIONS

1. In a mixing bowl, add the pork and flour and toss until the pork is coated.

2. In a large saucepan, add the oil and cook over medium-high heat until warm. Add the pork and cook for 5 minutes, or until evenly browned.

3. Remove the meat from the pan and set aside.

4. Reduce the heat to medium and add the butter. Add the onions and garlic and cook for 5 minutes, or until soft. Add the herbs and potatoes and cook for 5 minutes.

5. Add the red wine and cook for 5 minutes, or until reduced by half.

6. Add the stock and bring to a boil. Reduce heat so that the soup simmers, return the pork to the pan, cover, and cook for 20 minutes.

7. Add the apples and cook for 15 minutes.

8. Once the pork, apples, and potatoes are tender, season with salt and pepper and serve in warm bowls.

INGREDIENTS

14 GARLIC CLOVES, UNPEELED

½ TEASPOON CORIANDER SEEDS

½ TEASPOON CUMIN SEEDS

½ TEASPOON BLACK PEPPERCORNS

1 STAR ANISE POD

2 WHOLE CLOVES

¼ CUP LARD

1 LB. BONELESS, SKINLESS CHICKEN THIGHS

1 LB. BEEF CHUCK, CUBED

1 LB. PORK SHOULDER, CUBED

1 MEDIUM WHITE ONION, HALVED AND CHARRED

¼ TEASPOON DRIED MEXICAN OREGANO

½ TEASPOON ACHIOTE POWDER

¼ TEASPOON CINNAMON

2 BAY LEAVES

4 CUPS CHICKEN STOCK OR WATER

¾ CUP DICED SWEET POTATO

¾ CUP DICED CARROTS

¾ CUP DICED POTATO

¾ CUP DICED SQUASH

8 OZ. CABBAGE, QUARTERED

8 OZ. RIPENED PLANTAIN, SLICED ½ INCH THICK

½ CUP COOKED CHICKPEAS

CORN TORTILLAS, WARM, FOR SERVING

PUCHERO DE TRES CARNES

YIELD: **4 SERVINGS**

ACTIVE TIME: **1 HOUR**

TOTAL TIME: **1 HOUR AND 30 MINUTES**

DIRECTIONS

1. Place the garlic cloves in a dry skillet and toast them over medium heat until lightly charred in spots, about 10 minutes, turning occasionally. Remove from the pan and let the garlic cool slightly. When the garlic is cool enough to handle, peel and finely dice it.

2. Place the coriander seeds, cumin seeds, peppercorns, star anise, and cloves in the skillet and toast until fragrant, shaking the pan to keep them from burning. Use a mortar and pestle or a spice grinder to grind them to a fine powder.

3. Place some lard in a large saucepan and melt it over medium heat. Working with one protein at a time, add them to the pan and sear until browned all over. Remove the browned meats and set them aside. Add some of the remaining lard to the pan if it starts to look dry while searing the meat. When the chicken is cool enough to handle, chop it into cubes.

4. Add the onion, garlic, toasted spice powder, oregano, achiote powder, cinnamon, and bay leaves to the pan and cook until the onion is translucent, about 3 minutes. Return the meat to the pan along with any juices. Cover the mixture with stock and bring the soup to a simmer. Cook until the meat is very tender, about 1 hour.

5. Remove the proteins and strain the broth. Return the broth to the pan and bring it to a simmer. Working with one at a time, add the sweet potato, carrots, potatoes, squash, cabbage, and plantain to the pan and simmer until tender. Set the vegetables aside with the meat.

6. Season the broth with salt and add the chickpeas. Cook until warmed through.

7. Divide the meats and vegetables between the serving bowls. Ladle some broth into each and serve with tortillas.

QUICK
LAMB STEW

YIELD: **4 SERVINGS**

ACTIVE TIME: **15 MINUTES**

TOTAL TIME: **30 MINUTES**

INGREDIENTS

2 TABLESPOONS VEGETABLE OIL

1 ONION, PEELED AND CHOPPED

1 LB. LAMB LOIN, FAT REMOVED
 AND CUT INTO ½-INCH PIECES

2 GARLIC CLOVES

1 TABLESPOON CUMIN

1 TABLESPOON CHOPPED
 ROSEMARY LEAVES, PLUS 4 SPRIGS
 FOR GARNISH

2 (14 OZ.) CANS OF DICED
 TOMATOES

4 CUPS LAMB STOCK

2 POTATOES, PEELED AND CUT
 INTO ½-INCH PIECES

2 CUPS CHOPPED GREEN BEANS

JUICE OF 1 LEMON

SALT AND PEPPER, TO TASTE

DIRECTIONS

1. In a medium saucepan, add the oil and cook over medium heat.

2. When the oil is warm, add the onion and lamb and cook for 5 minutes, or until lamb is browned all over.

3. Add the garlic, cumin, rosemary, and tomatoes and cook for an additional 5 minutes.

4. Add the stock and potatoes, increase heat to high, and bring to a boil.

5. Reduce heat so that the soup simmers. Cook for 10 minutes, or until the potatoes are tender.

6. Add the green beans and cook for 5 minutes.

7. Season with lemon juice, salt, and pepper and serve in warmed bowls garnished with a sprig of rosemary.

ROCKY MOUNTAIN CHILI

YIELD: **4 TO 6 SERVINGS**

ACTIVE TIME: **30 MINUTES**

TOTAL TIME: **1 HOUR AND 30 MINUTES**

INGREDIENTS

1 TABLESPOON VEGETABLE OIL

1 ONION, CHOPPED

1 LB. GROUND TURKEY

2 GARLIC CLOVES, MINCED

1 TABLESPOON CHILI POWDER

1 BOUQUET GARNI (SEE PAGE 338)

4 TOMATOES, DICED

1 (14 OZ.) CAN TOMATO SAUCE

8 TABLESPOONS TOMATO PASTE

1 (14 OZ.) CAN KIDNEY BEANS

1 (14 OZ.) CAN WHITE BEANS

1 (14 OZ.) CAN BLACK BEANS

SALT AND PEPPER, TO TASTE

SHREDDED CHEDDAR CHEESE,
    FOR GARNISH

SOUR CREAM, FOR GARNISH

CHIVES, CHOPPED, FOR GARNISH

TO SERVE:

CORN BREAD (SEE PAGE 332)

DIRECTIONS

1. In a large saucepan, add the oil and cook over medium-high heat until warm.

2. Add the onion and ground turkey and cook for 5 minutes, or until meat has been browned.

3. Add the garlic and cook for 2 minutes, then add the chili powder, bouquet garni, tomatoes, tomato sauce, tomato paste, and beans. Bring to a boil, reduce heat so that the soup simmers, and cook for 20 minutes, or until the meat is cooked through.

4. Season with salt and pepper and ladle into warmed bowls. Serve with cornbread, shredded cheddar cheese, sour cream, and chopped chives.

SANTA FE CHILI WITH CORN BREAD

YIELD: **4 SERVINGS**

ACTIVE TIME: **45 MINUTES**

TOTAL TIME: **2 HOURS AND 30 MINUTES**

DIRECTIONS

1. In a large saucepan, add the oil and beef shanks and cook over medium heat for 5 minutes on each side, or until lightly browned.

2. Remove the beef shanks from the pan and set aside. Add the onion and cook for 3 minutes.

3. Add the corn, bell pepper, cumin, and garlic and cook for 3 minutes, or until the vegetables are soft.

4. Reduce heat and return the beef shanks to the pan. Add the tomato paste and stock and allow soup to simmer for 2 hours, or until the meat is tender.

5. Remove the beef shanks. Cut the meat from the bone and chop into ½-inch pieces. Return meat to the soup.

6. Add tomato and simmer for 10 minutes.

7. Skim any fat off the top of the soup. Add the red pepper flakes, Tabasco, salt, and pepper and serve in bowls with the Corn Bread and Spiced Butter.

CORN BREAD

1. Preheat the oven to 375°F.

2. In a mixer, combine the egg, milk, and oil and mix on low speed.

3. Meanwhile, sieve your dry ingredients together.

4. Slowly incorporate the dry mixture into the egg mixture.

5. Pour the batter into a buttered and floured 8-inch cast-iron pan. Place in oven and cook for 30 minutes, or until a cake tester or toothpick comes out clean.

SPICED BUTTER

1. Combine butter and spices in the bowl of a stand mixer and whip for 5 minutes.

2. Season to taste with salt and serve.

INGREDIENTS

1 TABLESPOON VEGETABLE OIL

1 LB. BEEF SHANKS, BONE IN

1 ONION, PEELED AND CHOPPED

1 CUP CORN KERNELS

½ CUP CHOPPED GREEN BELL
  PEPPER

½ TEASPOON GROUND CUMIN

2 GARLIC CLOVES, MINCED

1 TABLESPOON TOMATO PASTE

6 CUPS BEEF OR VEAL STOCK

1 TOMATO, CONCASSE (SEE
  PAGE 339)

⅛ TEASPOON RED PEPPER FLAKES

⅛ TEASPOON TABASCO

SALT AND PEPPER, TO TASTE

TO SERVE:

CORN BREAD

SPICED BUTTER

CORN BREAD

1 LARGE EGG

¾ CUP MILK

½ CUP VEGETABLE OIL

½ CUP SUGAR, PLUS 3 TABLESPOONS

1 CUP ALL-PURPOSE FLOUR

⅓ CUP CORNMEAL, PLUS 2
  TABLESPOONS

1 TEASPOON SALT

1 TEASPOON BAKING POWDER

SPICED BUTTER

1 CUP UNSALTED BUTTER,
  SOFTENED

1 TEASPOON CINNAMON

½ TEASPOON GROUND GINGER

¼ TEASPOON GROUND CLOVES

¼ TEASPOON NUTMEG

SALT, TO TASTE

INGREDIENTS

1 LB. CANNELLINI BEANS, SOAKED

2 LBS. CHICKEN THIGHS, BONED AND SKINNED, BONES RESERVED

2 BAY LEAVES

1 TABLESPOON KOSHER SALT

2 ROSEMARY SPRIGS

SALT AND PEPPER, TO TASTE

2 TABLESPOONS EXTRA-VIRGIN OLIVE OIL, PLUS MORE FOR DRIZZLING

1 YELLOW ONION, PEELED AND DICED

3 CARROTS, DICED

2 CELERY STALKS, DICED

1 YELLOW BELL PEPPER, SEEDED AND DICED

1 ORANGE BELL PEPPER, SEEDED AND DICED

3 GARLIC CLOVES, MINCED

1 TEASPOON CRUSHED RED PEPPER FLAKES

4 SMALL ROMA TOMATOES, DICED

2 TABLESPOONS CHOPPED SAGE

1½ OZ. ASIAGO CHEESE, GRATED

¼ CUP CHOPPED BASIL

SCALLIONS, CHOPPED, FOR GARNISH

TUSCAN CHICKEN & WHITE BEAN STEW

YIELD: **4 TO 6 SERVINGS**

ACTIVE TIME: **30 TO 45 MINUTES**

TOTAL TIME: **1 HOUR AND 45 MINUTES**

DIRECTIONS

1. Drain the cannellini beans and rinse them. Place in the Dutch oven, cover with water, and cook over medium heat. Add the chicken bones, bay leaves, salt, and the rosemary. Cover and cook, stirring occasionally, for about 1 hour, until the beans are soft and starting to fall apart.

2. While the beans are cooking, season the chicken with salt and pepper and set aside.

3. When the beans are done, pour them into a bowl. Remove the chicken bones, rosemary sprigs, and the bay leaves. Place the Dutch oven back on the stove and add the olive oil. Warm over medium heat and then add the chicken thighs. Cook for about 5 minutes on each side until the chicken is cooked through. Remove from the pot and let cool. When cool, dice the chicken.

4. Place the onion, carrots, celery, bell peppers, garlic, red pepper flakes, tomatoes, and sage in the pot and cook for 20 minutes until the vegetables are soft and have released their juices. While the vegetables are cooking, transfer the beans to a blender and puree. Place the beans back in the pot and then stir in the Asiago and basil. Season with salt and pepper and cook for 7 to 10 minutes until the cheese is melted. Return the diced chicken to the pot and cook until heated through. Drizzle with additional olive oil, garnish with scallions if desired, and serve.

WHITE CHICKEN CHILI

YIELD: **6 SERVINGS**

ACTIVE TIME: **15 MINUTES**

TOTAL TIME: **24 HOURS**

INGREDIENTS

1 LB. WHITE BEANS, SOAKED OVERNIGHT AND DRAINED

¼ CUP VEGETABLE OIL

6 BONELESS, SKINLESS CHICKEN THIGHS

1 MEDIUM WHITE ONION, MINCED

3 GARLIC CLOVES, MINCED

1 CUP SOFRITO

1 (7 OZ.) CAN DICED, MILD GREEN CHILIES

6 CUPS CHICKEN STOCK

1 TABLESPOON WHITE PEPPER

3 TABLESPOONS DRIED OREGANO

1 TABLESPOON CUMIN

1 TABLESPOON ADOBO SEASONING

SALT AND PEPPER, TO TASTE

DIRECTIONS

1. Place the beans in a Dutch oven and cover with water. Bring to a boil, reduce heat to medium-low, and cover the pot. Cook for 45 minutes to 1 hour until the beans are tender. Drain and set the beans aside.

2. Place the pot back on the stove and warm the oil over medium-high heat. Add the chicken and cook for 5 minutes on each side. Remove the chicken and set aside.

3. Add the onion and garlic to the pot and cook until the onions are translucent, about 5 to 7 minutes.

4. Add the Sofrito and green chilies and cook, stirring occasionally, for 5 minutes.

5. Return the beans and the chicken to the Dutch oven. Add the remaining ingredients, reduce the heat to medium, cover, and cook for 1 hour.

6. Remove the cover, stir, and cook for an additional 30 minutes to 1 hour, until the chili has thickened and the chicken is falling apart.

TECHNIQUES

BOUQUET GARNI

Cut a 2-foot section of butcher twine. Tie one side of the rope around the herbs and tightly knot it. Attach the other end of the twine to the pot. For the purpose of this book we will use the traditional preparation of bay leaf and fresh sprigs of thyme and parsley.

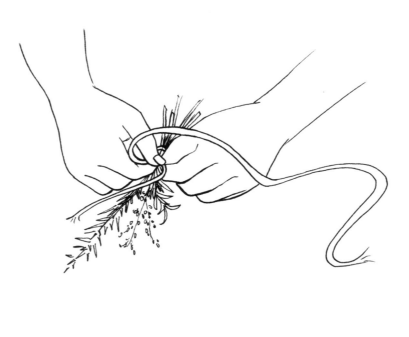

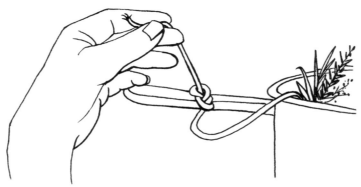

TOMATO CONCASSE

Boil enough water for a tomato to be submerged and add a pinch of salt. While it is heating, prepare an ice bath and score the top of the tomato with a paring knife, taking care not to cut into the meat of the tomato. Place the tomato in the boiling water for 30 seconds, or until the skin begins to blister. Carefully remove it from the boiling water and place it in the ice bath. Once the tomato is cool, remove it from the ice bath and use a paring knife to peel the skin off, starting at the scored top. Cut the tomato into quarters, remove the seeds, and cut.

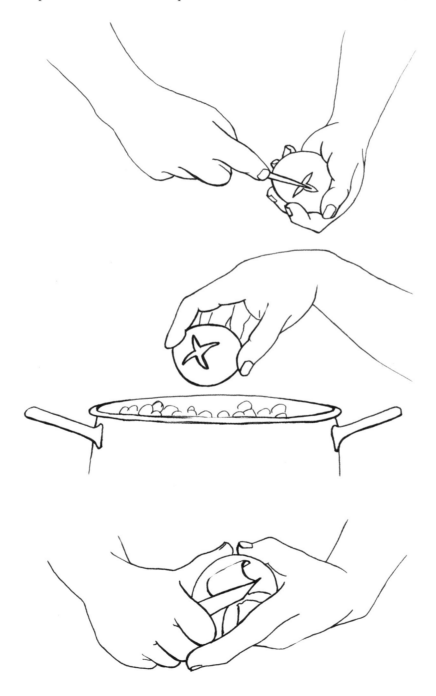

SACHET D'EPICES

Cut a 4-inch square of cheesecloth and a 12-inch piece of butcher twine. Place 3 parsley stems, ¼ teaspoon. thyme leaves, ½ bay leaf, ¼ teaspoon. cracked peppercorns, and ½ garlic clove, minced, in the middle of the cheesecloth and lift each corner to create a purse. Tie one side of the twine around the corners and make a knot. Tie the other side of the twine to the handle of your pot and then toss the sachet d'epice in.

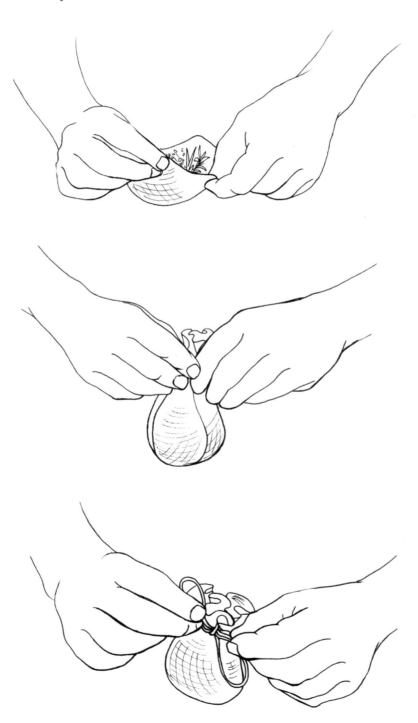

FILLING AND SHAPING WONTONS

When working with wonton dough, you want to leave it covered until you're going to use them. When you are ready, lay a few wrappers out on your work surface and place your filling in the center. Dip your finger into some water and wet the edge of the wonton wrapper. Not too much water, or the dough will become sticky and unworkable. Take two opposite corners and lift until they meet. Secure with a little pinch, and then lift the two remaining corners, one at a time.

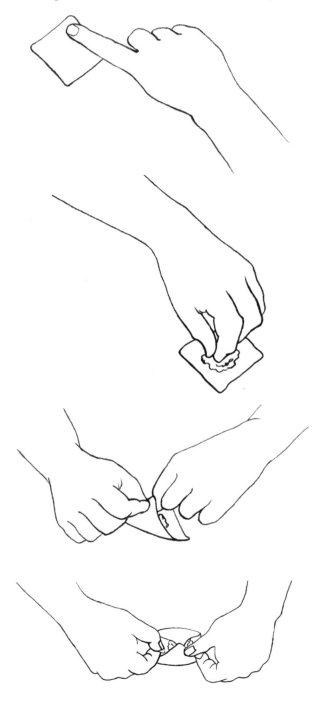

PITA BREAD

YIELD: **8 SERVINGS**

ACTIVE TIME: **1 HOUR**

TOTAL TIME: **3 HOURS**

INGREDIENTS

1 CUP LUKEWARM WATER

3 TEASPOONS DRY ACTIVE YEAST

3 TEASPOONS WHITE SUGAR

1¾ CUPS ALL-PURPOSE WHITE FLOUR

1 CUP WHEAT FLOUR

1 TABLESPOON KOSHER SALT

DIRECTIONS

1. In a large bowl combine the water, yeast, and sugar. Let sit for 15 minutes or so, until the water is foamy and bubbling. Add the flours and salt, mixing until the flour and water form a dough. Sprinkle with flour when necessary to work the dough. Knead the dough for 1 minute or so, just until the ball is smooth and uniform; it does not need to be kneaded otherwise. Set aside, covered by a towel or plastic wrap, for 2 hours.

2. Preheat the oven to 500°F and place a cast-iron pan or upside-down baking sheet in the oven.

3. Separate the dough into 8 even pieces and ball them up. One at a time, on a floured surface, press the ball down and then, using a rolling pin, roll into a flat surface about ¼-inch thick.

4. Bake the pitas, 1 at a time. It will take approximately 3 minutes to puff up and 5 minutes or so to brown slightly and be done baking. Serve hot or keep at room temperature.

METRIC CONVERSIONS

U.S. Measurement	Approximate Metric Liquid Measurement	Approximate Metric Dry Measurement
1 teaspoon	5 ml	5 g
1 tablespoon or ½ ounce	15 ml	14 g
1 ounce or ⅛ cup	30 ml	29 g
¼ cup or 2 ounces	60 ml	57 g
⅓ cup	80 ml	76 g
½ cup or 4 ounces	120 ml	113 g
⅔ cup	160 ml	151 g
¾ cup or 6 ounces	180 ml	170 g
1 cup or 8 ounces or ½ pint	240 ml	227 g
1½ cups or 12 ounces	350 ml	340 g
2 cups or 1 pint or 16 ounces	475 ml	454 g
3 cups or 1½ pints	700 ml	680 g
4 cups or 2 pints or 1 quart	950 ml	908 g

INDEX